The Extraordinary Life
of a Versatile Person

The Extraordinary Life of a Versatile Person

Adrian Seager

Matador
Unit E2 Airfield Business Park,
Harrison Road, Market Harborough,
Leicestershire. LE16 7UL
Tel: 0116 279 2299
Email: books@troubador.co.uk
Web: www.troubador.co.uk/matador
Twitter: @matadorbooks

ISBN 978 1 80514 093 1

British Library Cataloguing in Publication Data.
A catalogue record for this book is available from the British Library.

Printed by TJ Books Limited, Padstow, UK
Typeset in 12pt Minion Pro by Troubador Publishing Ltd, Leicester, UK

Matador is an imprint of Troubador Publishing Ltd

Contents

Preface

This is the story of an unusually varied, challenging and precarious working life.

It encompasses numerous and widely different types of work in one lifetime, including the demoralising effect of being unemployed, recovery from setbacks and the eventual realisation that, for years, I had been in the wrong job.

Collapsing in midlife was a shock that served as a semicolon in the line of events, leading to a significant change of direction.

The enforced period of rest provided a window through which life was assessed objectively. The view was that life had been driving me at an ever-increasing rate. Fate had taken a hand and would lead me to take control of my life going forwards.

The control would be in the form of a determination to work at a pace that would allow mind and body to manage the energy necessary to live a balanced existence.

The opportunity to turn my back on the world of manufacturing and commerce occurred when qualifying as a chiropodist and, later, as a registered reflexologist, which led to establishing a private practice.

For years, family and friends said I should chronicle my nomadic professional life and it is their encouragement that has led to this book.

Acknowledgements

Grateful thanks to my daughter-in-law, Angie, for producing the typed version from handwritten drafts and notes. Her patience, cheerfulness and encouragement has been my good fortune.

Throughout the process of writing, my wife, Norma, not only kept me awake, fed and watered, but also acted as a first critique and guardian of grammar. Thank you.

My children and grandchildren kept a watching brief from time to time and supplied some useful ideas for which I am grateful. They will not begrudge a special thank you to Hannah, who transposed the numerous end photographs into digital format with great patience and attention to detail.

The idea to record my professional wanderings into a book arose from conversations with my long-standing friend, Tony Porter. His support and interest throughout were great encouragement.

I thank the many former work colleagues and friends for their help and support throughout my lifetime.

Finally, a posthumous acknowledgement to my Labrador dog, Paddy, for the alarm he barked when I needed it most.

chapter one

The Family Background

Our family background was in glove manufacturing, for which Yeovil was known. There were a number of thriving glove factories in the town and it was the reason that the local football club came to be known as the 'The Glovers'.

At one time, my grandad, William Seager, employed nearly two hundred people in his factory at 32 Seaton Road, Yeovil. It was a tall building that was much later occupied by British Telecommunications Ltd. During the successful years, Grandad supplied a number of well-known retailers, including Selfridges of London. However, in 1929, it all came to grief – the grief of liquidation and the sale and distribution of all assets that had residual value.

Today, it can be difficult to understand – when we read, or watch on television – successful companies collapsing. How could it happen? Seager's factory's demise was a classic example of how events beyond and outside a company's control can overcome its ability to trade. Often, it is due to a change in the market upon which it depends. Occasionally, it can be a consequence of government action. For example: when a government department is your main or sole outlet and the decision is taken, at short notice, to end the contract as part of treasury cutbacks, leaving insufficient time to seek alternative markets. University gurus would say the company should have diversified, but a small company will grab the chance of a lucrative contract because it's a 'big step' that must be grasped. However, this means you have to put all your resources into satisfying the requirements of that customer. Diversification will have to be for another day. This is how my grandad's company went into liquidation, necessitating the appointment of an official receiver.

Yet he had qualities necessary to create any business – determination, courage and stubbornness – as well as to overcome all sceptics (rarely in short supply) and the bureaucratic hurdles that seem to spring up when you least suspect it. However, these same qualities exercised at the wrong time and in the wrong way can be detrimental – as will be seen later.

Grandad started the business in 1898, at the age of thirty-one, with a cash capital of £120 (the official receiver's observation). He built it up on a reputation for quality and for being a man of his word. In today's language, he would 'tell it how it is'. He was, in many ways, a perfectionist and this meant he could be a hard taskmaster.

During the 1920s, he met a tailor who was cutting cloth for men's suits – not one at a time but in batches, by stacking the cloth like a sandwich. This enabled a number of pieces of cloth to be cut simultaneously. Grandad saw the potential of using a similar method of cutting leather. He began cutting stretched leather skins in stacked batches, increasing the rate of production.

All was well initially, with a gradual increase in employment to the business. Then, the government allowed cheap goods to be imported from Japan, including gloves. On the face of it, the government was lowering prices and helping people cope with the years of depression. However, while helping the general population, some businesses were adversely affected, including the Seager family business. Timing is as an important aspect of any business.

Increased production meant increased sales; excellent, but when cheap imports undercut your product, the finished goods go into stock until the market stabilises. This is what Grandad did because he argued that quality will always win and people would find the cheap imported gloves would not last or keep their shape and so sales of his gloves would recover. Meanwhile, cash flow and paying the wages of employees became critical, requiring the continual support of the mortgage from the bank. But the bank would not support Grandad's reasoning. The slide was beginning; the gloves did not sell because of government action, however well intended it may have been, which led to a serious drop in the market. This was the dilemma. His two elder sons advised him to drop his prices and cut his losses. He would not hear of it and argued that, in six months, things would recover – his stubborn streak.

Meanwhile, there were mortgages on the factory premises, secured against the family home – an imposing house and grounds at 31 Hendford Hill – and other property in the town, adding to the growing financial crisis. This had crystallised into how to fill the financial gap until sales recovered.

For the next eighteen months, the business ticked over (the receiver's phrase) as stocks continued to accumulate. Grandad had to lay off employees who had been loyal to him. He had no choice and it upset him. He sold his three cars (he was one of the first in the area to own a car) and, in desperation, speculated in stocks and shares in an attempt to save the company, his family and his employees, by overcoming the cash flow and meet the legal liabilities of his cumulative debt.

The combination of a large loss on one particular stock, together with a simultaneous writ for payment from one of his largest creditors, proved too much. He had to accept defeat and the company went into receivership.

Grandad was fifty-two and a bitter man. Bitter because the bank had refused an extension of the overdraft facility and, in his opinion, refused to give him sufficient time to turn the business around or to listen to his plans to rescue the company.

The sight of the bailiffs removing every stick of furniture and stripping his former home bare was a tear-jerking experience my father would never forget. Neither could he forget the distress it caused his parents, particularly his mother. I believe it was these events that caused him to be cautious for the rest of his life. In all probability, it was a major factor to him encouraging me to apply for an engineering apprenticeship. "Make sure you have a good foundation of knowledge and skill to fall back on" was his echo of the past. The fact he referred to it as something 'to fall back on' spoke volumes. Security was a key factor in seeking long-term employment with a well-known and established organisation.

Dad was a modest man and, for that reason, he did not get the recognition I believe he deserved. It is for this reason that I outline his career in detail here.

In the years before the company failure, my father had moved to Gloster Aircraft to gain further design experience to that gained while at Westland Aircraft. In the 1930s, it was common for designers to move around, often in step with any new order being won by their next employer. He obtained lodgings at Lansdown Road, Cheltenham, along with another young Gloster Aircraft design draftsman, George Dowty, later to become Sir George Dowty (1901–1974) for his service to the aero industry with aircraft undercarriages used throughout the world.

He used to invite my father around to a nearby lock-up garage to show him what he was building and share the work on a sprung undercarriage he was developing – this superseded the hydraulic versions that came later and are a familiar feature on most of the world's airlines. They spent many evenings in the garage. When Sir George (George, in those days) decided to take a chance and launch his company, he wanted Dad to join him, but the dilemma at the family factory, the recall of a loan and his forthcoming marriage made it impossible for Dad to take the financial risk. It was the most difficult decision he had to make and one of his greatest regrets. Their friendship dwindled gradually as George Dowty grew into a limited liability company and the large organisation it became.

Dad returned to Westland Aircraft (Petters, in those days), for whom he worked, with great enthusiasm, for almost fifty years. For a variety of reasons, he 'just missed out' on two or three occasions in his career – not least when he invented the self-tapping screw. The law then was that you could not claim you had had the idea in your own time, hence such inventions were deemed to belong to your employer.

Between 1926 and 1934, he worked directly with Captain G.T.R. Hill on the pioneering design of various types of pterodactyl tailless aircraft – believed to be the first tailless aircraft to actually fly. But government support was not forthcoming. Later, he was assistant chief designer for 'Teddy' Petter (of the Petter dynasty) who was responsible for the Lysander, which flew just eleven months after pencil was put to paper! It is amazing what was achieved during the demands of World War II.

He also assisted in the design of the Whirlwind, Welkin and prototype Canberra bomber, which Mr Petter took with him when he went to Folland Aircraft, Preston. He worked on the Wyvern naval strike aircraft – the last fixed-wing aircraft produced at the Yeovil factory. The Lysander, Whirlwind, Welkin and Wyvern were all test flown by the well-known test pilot and author, the late Harald Penrose. He worked closely with Dad throughout the development of these aircraft and they remained good friends in their retirement. The Welkin aircraft was a high-altitude machine used for the design and development of cabin air-conditioning, which became Normalair Limited (later Normalair-Garrett).

Dad was a chartered engineer and life member of the Royal Aeronautical Society and was instrumental in the founding of a local branch of the society. He maintained a keen interest in the industry and was still giving lectures in his eighties, which took him to various parts of England. He never tired of helping others from his wealth of experience, sometimes at his cost.

He was responsible for much of the design work of the Lysander, which played a prominent role in World War II. Its short take-off and landing distance made it ideal for dropping or collecting agents behind enemy lines.

In retirement, Dad responded each year to an invitation to speak at the Strathallan Museum, near Auchterarder, which had a collection of aircraft, including a Lysander they took pride in. Dad's detailed knowledge was greatly appreciated.

He returned for a number of years to give illustrated talks and to share his first-hand experience until the journey from Somerset to Scotland became a little too much for him. In gratitude, the Society made him a life member. Unfortunately, the Strathallan Aircraft Collection closed on 7th August 1980, following the sale of most of its aircraft.

My paternal grandmother, typical of her era, was a loving mother to my father and his four brothers and two sisters. It was hardly surprising that they occupied a large, detached house at the top of Hendford Hill Yeovil.

My maternal grandmother, born Lottie Hallet (married name Martin), was a tailoress and worked in a major outfitter in Yeovil before the demands of World War II. Because of her background, she was employed during the war at Westland Aircraft to make the fabric covering for the wings and tail planes of aircraft before many of those items were replaced by metal covering and other materials were used in place of leather trimmings.

She was a kind, determined lady who was widowed when my mother, Freda, and Uncle Norman were aged only three and one respectively. She must have overcome the dreadful shock of being widowed so young. Tragically, my grandfather died when he fell from a ladder while working on the top guttering of their terraced house.

I came across her marriage certificate in some family archives, which proved she got married while pregnant with her first child, my mother. In those days, a scandal had to be avoided. This, no doubt, would have come to light only if I had become sufficiently well-known as to have been invited to feature in the television programme *Who Do You Think You Are?*!

Grandmother continued working until the time when, cycling home for lunch, a German aircraft chose to dive and spray the road with machine gunfire, killing and injuring some of her work colleagues cycling beside her. She never really got over the shock and grief of this incident and left work soon afterwards. She lived to over one hundred years old, ending her life well cared for in a neighbouring residential home where she made a never-to-be-forgotten remark, whispered in my ear, "Look around you. I get bored because they are all so old."

Of course, she was the eldest, but was mentally active until pneumonia got the better of her – though not before she had realised a long-held ambition of flying in a Westland helicopter in celebration of her hundredth birthday. Long may she rest in peace.

My grandfather's car (reg YA 1349) at his home at the top of Hendford Hill, Yeovil, 12th May 1925. This picture illustrates the lifestyle my grandfather enjoyed before his company's demise and the resulting shock on the whole family.

chapter two

The Early Years

Here I am, in my early eighties, lucky to have reached this stage and looking forward to tomorrow with its promise of uncertainty and freshness. Waking each morning has become a pleasant surprise!

From the age of five, when war broke out in September 1939, until the age of eleven, I grew up during World War II in an atmosphere that was a mixture of fear, apprehension and communal cheerfulness. Good humour was widespread, not the doom and gloom that is too prevalent today. There was a neighbourliness like no other since that time. Each morning, or after each air raid, people emerged from their homes and shelters, curious to see what was left standing.

I was born in Yeovil Maternity Hospital in April 1934. It was the year Henry Cotton won the British Open Golf Championship; Fred Perry won the men's single title at Wimbledon; the ocean liner *The Queen Mary* was launched from Southampton; the Mersey Tunnel was opened by King George V; and Bridgette Bardot and Sophia Loren were born. It was also the year Sir Edward Elgar died. There is a memorial statue of him in Worcester, near the city's Cathedral. It is hardly surprising that my arrival went unnoticed, apart from our immediate family. My birth, and many others, took place in a dedicated maternity hospital. Sadly, Britain's post-war urge to modernise meant it was demolished to make way for a large and frustratingly busy roundabout serving five diverse roads.

1934 also saw the disruption of London's traffic by the introduction of pedestrian crossings in the city. It was intended to reduce road casualties – maybe the inhabitants of that time were not as fleet of foot as those of today.

In March of the same year, the driving test was introduced. Previously, the only requirement for drivers of motorised vehicles was an unsupported declaration of physical fitness, given by anyone to anyone over the age of seventeen.

Mandatory speed limits of thirty miles per hour in built-up areas became law in 1935. With the interim improvement in vehicle design, construction, performance and braking capability, it is amazing that the speed limit has remained unchanged from the time of its introduction. There seems to be a doctrine today to reduce speed, while always ignoring the greater need for concentration and anticipation by drivers, plus the need for all road users, including pedestrians, to apply the same discipline.

I am an only child, and some psychologists might claim that makes me inclined to be selfish; instead, life has made me self-sufficient and, in my early years, a shy person. By nature, I am not a loner. Beyond the age of about eight, it has been easy to make friends and there is pleasure in starting a conversation, often finding that the recipient will respond and open up.

It is a strange fact of life how some events in our childhood remain a vivid memory. As a five-year-old, I remember watching my father leave for work. He rode a Francis Barnett two-stroke motorbike, which blew out copious exhaust fumes and made sufficient noise to be noticed by the neighbours. His outfit included a leather jacket, matching cap, gauntlets and a scarf, all donned before take-off down the lane and around the corner at the end of our lane and out of sight.

Afterwards and after breakfast, it would be back to our good-sized garden and riding around the footpath on a tricycle that served as a pretend fire engine, bus or ambulance depending on the imagination at the time. I still recall passing one perennial plant, a cornflower, which had a rather strange perfume and seemed to flower forever.

We lived in a small, detached, two-bedroomed bungalow on the edge of town, looking out onto a market garden and fields beyond. In the distance, we could see the Fleet Air Arm base and aerodrome at Yeovilton, now known for its museum. There were no street lights or pavement and the lane, Coombe Lane, was surfaced with pink stone chippings thrown onto wet tar and rolled in by large steamrollers. I can clearly recall the combined smell of tar and steam and the rattle of that large steamroller.

The facilities of our home would be strange to people of the twenty-first century. Our bungalow had a dining room with an adjacent kitchen. To call it a kitchen is misleading.

It was the size of a large wardrobe and had a kitchen sink and a wooden draining board, with a hand pump above it to enable us to draw water from the well in the garden. A boiler was in one corner. This was not a central heating boiler; it was a large enamel-covered iron cylinder on three legs with gas burners beneath the base. On wash days (Mondays), clothes were put in the boiler; it was then filled with water, the gas burner was lit, and the water was heated to boiling and stirred occasionally with a wooden pole. It had a circular thick wooden cover to hold in the steam. When washed, the clothes, linen and bed clothes etc. were removed and wrung out by hand before going through the wooden rollers of a large upright ringer. My mother had to wind the large metal wheel on the ringer, which turned the wooden rollers that pulled the clothes through, squashing out the surplus water into the attached timber tray as they rotated.

Only then would the items be pegged out on the clothes line in the garden. The clothes line also had some engineering. It comprised a rope stretched between two vertical wooden poles that were fixed into the ground; there was also a central pole with a pulley-wheel, so that the line, heavy with damp washing, could be hauled up sufficiently high enough for the clothes to swing clear of the ground and dry in the fresh air.

Adjacent to the kitchen was a larder, rarely seen now and far removed from kitchen designs. This one had a small window of perforated fine zinc gauge, not glass. This allowed fresh air to ventilate the space twenty-four hours a day. A marble shelf kept the jug of milk cool. The jug was covered with a damp muslin cloth, so that the evaporation helped the cooling process. The milkman called every day, scooping the milk from a milk churn into people's milk jugs. This door-to-door service meant the milk was always fresh and could be kept fresh until the next day.

Eggs were another product to be kept fresh and germ-free. They were kept in large earthenware jars filled with a white preservative called waterglass. The eggs were placed carefully into this liquid and stayed fresh until needed. Similarly, carrots, beetroot, parsnips and other home-grown root crops were stored in boxes or huge jars filled with dry sand. They lasted through most of the winter months. We had to be self-sufficient.

Self-sufficiency was forced upon us by the war. The only imports were from the brave efforts of our merchant navy, which ferried to and fro across the Atlantic Ocean, constantly at risk from the German U-boats (submarines). Their priority was carrying food and other essentials needed for the war effort, while surviving submarine or aircraft attacks.

People with gardens kept chickens for their eggs and the widespread slogan of that time was 'Dig for Victory', which was on display around the whole country. This meant that every spare plot of land, however small, was dug up and planted with potatoes and vegetables to feed families. In addition, iron railings surrounding or fronting private or public property were removed for the war effort; this included those on a small wall in front of my grandmother's garden wall – they were simply cut off at the base and taken away. There was little doubt that we were all in it together.

These grim days had some macabre attractions. I remember, in 1940, watching an aerial dogfight between our fighters and some enemy planes high in the sky on a glorious summer's day. We watched from a dry ditch that bordered a nearby playing field and in which we had taken cover. The crackle of gunfire and the patterns of vapour trails in the clear blue sky as the aircraft weaved and dived was both fascinating and a little frightening.

Additional protection in the ditch was provided by our evacuee Mrs Feather, who was billeted with us with her daughter throughout the war years and became an extended part of our family. On this frightening occasion, she instinctively chose to lay over the two of us until danger had passed. She was a substantial lady whose weight was a minor threat to our survival, but under the circumstances was the least of our worries.

In the war years, there was a national evacuation scheme whereby children deemed to be in danger zones were moved to areas of the country thought to be safe from air raids. Some children were accompanied by their parent or guardian, but very many were on their own and struggled to adapt to their new and strange surroundings. No doubt today they would have been supported by counsellors.

There were lighter moments to take our minds off the serious situation that the country was in. The winters of the 1940s was colder than those of fifty or so years later. This enabled us to enjoy the frost and snow. Frost made fascinating patterns on bedroom windows in the early mornings. There was no central heating, just one small open coal fire in the corner of the bedroom, which was rarely lit to save coal.

The whole family and neighbours would gather at a hilltop, just along from our home, to whizz from the top to bottom on home-made toboggans. Bedtime gave way to the joy of sledging down the slope in the moonlight. Severe frost often produced a clear sky. The longer we stayed out after dark, the colder it got and the faster the slope became. It was wonderful, carefree and fun, with no health and safety to put a brake on it in those self-reliant days.

There was so much fun that on one particularly cold night, with the snow glistening in the bright moonlight, there was quite a large gathering enjoying sliding down the slope and trudging back up again to the top. The small crowd was of adults as well as children. There may have been more adults than children as the evening wore on.

My grandmother was among them and excitement of the moment caused her to have a go down the slope on the family sledge. Off she went, dressed in a warm overcoat, a scarf and a prominent hat with a feather in it. As she gathered speed, and because she had chosen to sit bolt upright rather than lie face-down on the sledge, this long feather flapped in the slipstream to the amusement of her 'audience'. She was well into her sixties, which, in the 1940s, was considered much too old to do such daring deeds. She drew spontaneous applause from all who witnessed my flying granny.

It was a pleasure and good luck to grow up in a rural area with fields and a wood, in which we built dens either on the ground, under the ground or in the lower branches of trees. Those days of freedom and little responsibility, before leaving school and beginning an engineering apprenticeship, seemed to pass all too quickly.

Up until the age of eight, I attended a small kindergarten run by a married couple, who had the knack of combining discipline with an almost parental kindness. There were only eight boys and girls. We attended from 9am until midday and they taught us a great deal in the homely environment of their large, detached cottage. They taught us so well that when entering the prep school of Crewkerne Grammar School, I was ahead of most of my classmates – except in spelling, which remains a personal weakness to this day. I blame the peculiarities of the English language – how can 'rough' be pronounced as 'ruff'?

This kindergarten was where my wife and I met, and the memories of that happy school include the smell of the place. It was a mix of paper (like the smell of printed gloss paper), crayons, polish and the scent from the ever-present vase of fresh flowers. You could not help feeling thoroughly at home, happy and relaxed. The curriculum included practice at writing between lines, with the capital letter written properly in the style of the day. A pride in the clarity and neatness of presentation was encouraged at all times. Each day started with a short burst of mental arithmetic, just adding and subtraction in the initial stages to 'wake our brains up'. We enjoyed learning because the teacher made it fun. The twelve times tables were learnt by rote and tested. There was pleasure and confidence in the routine and there was discipline. On arrival, we changed into soft shoes for indoors and hung our outer garments on our designated coat hooks. Courtesy and good manners were taught, supporting that taught by our parents. It was a process for preparing us for the way of life that existed in the late 1930s and on into the 1950s.

Aged eight, I took an entrance exam, was interviewed by the headmaster in the presence of my parents and accepted into the preparatory school within Crewkerne Grammar School. The school was an impressive building on the hill overlooking the market town of Crewkerne in Somerset. Founded in 1499 by a monk, John De Combe, it had a proud history and lasted until a Labour government closed it in favour of a school built on part of the old playing field. This school replaced our school, and neighbouring Ilminster and Chard, to form an all-embracing comprehensive school.

My early days at the grammar school were unhappy. It was a shock to change from starting at 9am at a school just down the road to a school that was nine miles away, which meant catching a bus at 8am in the town, 1.5 miles from home. It was also a shock to move from a group of eight children into a vastly different and much larger environment.

It was a shock because I had to overcome my real fear of heights, as the prep classroom was situated at the highest point of the school building, on the fourth floor. To get to it, you had to climb the concrete spiral stairway that was edged by a cast-iron, open-weave balustrade, which allowed an open view all the way down to the floor of the main entrance floor below. Before dismissing me as a tearful wimp, which I was in those initial few days, you must understand that we lived in a two-bedroomed bungalow, so height was never a problem or an experience.

In the following years, and certainly throughout senior school, I became as much of a menace as the rest of my friends and enjoyed playing for the school rugby team, as well as cricket and hockey. As a day boy in a boarding school, we had to attend on Saturday mornings, so in the autumn term – when rugby was played on Wednesday afternoons and school matches on Saturday afternoons – it became a six-day week, particularly on away games when it meant coming home late.

We 'Yeovil lads' had to catch the early bus at 8am, which meant leaving home at 7.30am and not arriving back in town until 5pm. For me, there was a 1.5 mile walk home after this, making it a long day, made even longer by homework. Why did I not board full-time? Because there were limited places and my parents could not afford the extra cost. Places to board were few and many of the boarders came from far and wide because rural Crewkerne was seen to be a safe area in wartime, so there was a large proportion of boys from the London and Bristol areas.

This kind of school life meant that, other than school holidays, there was little opportunity to make friends locally. It was not until I left school that it was possible to have friends inside and outside of working hours, yet I have many happy memories of school life, mostly in my early teens by which time there was a feeling of confidence that was lacking in my early years.

The Old Crewkernians Association does a splendid job of keeping many of us in touch. At one gathering I attended, there was an amusing meeting with an old school friend. We did not recognise each other at first and had to be introduced by a third person. The conversation went something like this, "Oh, I can see who you are now, but I remember you as a short, fat guy", which caused much laughter. I explained he was quite correct. Until I was fourteen, I was 4ft 11 and then the pituitary gland must have kicked in because from fourteen to sixteen I grew to 5ft 10, or 5ft 9.5 as the Forces Medical Board insisted later.

The chubbiness meant that I was always picked for the front row in rugby and was duly squashed. My new slimline version gave me more speed and a move to wing or full back, as I was able to kick long distances with either foot, but never at the same time.

My time at school ended in a way that was familiar. It was by sitting the School Certificate set by Cambridge University in 1950, the last one before being replaced by the General Certificate of Secondary Education (GCSE). To gain a school certificate required a pass in six subjects, including English language, without which you would not be awarded the certificate. Unfortunately, during the written language examination, I was unwell. I had to put my hand up and be escorted outside of the gymnasium building in which the examination was held, only to be physically sick and too ill to continue.

It was no surprise that I failed the written language exam, while gaining passes in five additional subjects. The headmaster, with supporting evidence from the master invigilating at the time, made a written request to Cambridge University Examination Board to let me resit the English Language paper because, as was learned subsequently, the 'failure' was by a few percentages only. But to no avail, which meant a year in the sixth form and a retake. In this case, I sat the new national GCSE and passed, albeit a year too late to go on to the Higher School Certificate – the gateway to university. Because of that lost year, I was now seventeen, too old to stay on at school and facing national service on reaching eighteen.

This presented a dilemma. National service was obligatory for all men over eighteen years of age – two years in one of the three services. Given free choice, my wish was to be a medical doctor or a vet. Both required a high school certificate for entry, for which I might have been deferred from national service until qualifying. My parents could not afford the long training associated with either profession, which concentrated the mind when deciding where to go from here. Against that background, the choice was a five-year engineering apprenticeship at Westland Aircraft, Yeovil.

The dilemma between school, the looming national service and work was resolved by my medical examination in Exeter, where I reported in August 1959. After measurements of height and weight were taken, and the routine strip and cough, I was graded officially as 'iii Three' due to my flat feet and, therefore, was not fit enough for national service.

There was a lighter side to the process. I still have my GRADE GUARD NS55 document that was issued with the results, which is stored at home in a drawer. There is a paragraph printed on it that reads, 'The roman numeral denoting the man's Grade (with number also spelt out) will be entered in RED ink by the chairman himself'. The chairman's name? Martin – Mum's maiden surname and, of course, my grandmother's married name. A strange coincidence and I have his autograph! The detail on the back of the card under the heading of 'DESCRIPTION OF MAN' reads: 'date-of-birth; height; colour of eyes (brown); colour of hair (brown).

Another reason for entering engineering was that I knew of no other avenue. In 1951, there was very little guidance or information about careers given in schools. When you left secondary education, you were stepping out into the unknown. The only time it was mentioned in the fifth year at school was when a teacher asked each of us in turn, "What do you want to do when you finish school?" This was the limit of their interest. They seemed content to get us through the School Certificate and Higher School Certificate and guiding us towards a university – job done. The alternative was to be released into the wide world like fledglings from a nest; some flew far, some did quite well and some not so well.

In the post-war period, entry to university was demanding and places were limited. There were bursaries for the bright ones, but grants were not available. There was an excellent scheme whereby servicemen returning from war service could obtain government support to gain or complete a university degree. It gave them the chance of completing studies interrupted by their time in the services.

The country was recovering from the cost and material damage of the war. It was many years later that a news bulletin told us the country had paid off the vast cost of these hostilities. Subsequently, we became involved in other hostilities – Egypt (the Suez Canal), the Falklands, Iraq etc. – so the country carries a huge debt to this day. We never seem to learn from history.

From 2010 onwards, much political attention has been given throughout the country to develop a skill-base alongside academia and technology, computerised systems and space exploration. The need for physical and machine skills tends to be overlooked and undervalued in the market for keen and able young people. It is when there is domestic electrical failure or a leaking water pipe that essential skills and knowledge receives our full attention and focuses the mind on what really matters.

The government's answer to skill shortage is to encourage apprenticeships as a worthwhile alternative to university degrees. This is history repeating itself. It is a repeat of many apprenticeships that existed when I was a teenager in the 1950s. Westland Aircraft Ltd, as it was known at the time, ran an excellent scheme. You joined on probation as an office boy and were attached to a department until there was a space for you on an intake into the company's on-site training school.

The apprenticeship was not cheap labour, as is sometimes claimed in parliamentary debates. It was an opportunity to earn a wage for the first time, while learning practical engineering skills alongside further education in technology. It was also the chance to mature by standing your ground among adults and overcoming some of the pranks they would play on you – like, "Go and get me some monkey grease, son."

Written reports were made every six months; a copy was held by the company and one was posted to your parent or guardian.

There was also the social aspect, thanks to the various clubs and activities within the company's sports and social club. We were provided with an environment in which we could adjust to the new adult world beyond school. Though we did not realise it at the time, the social mixing allowed us to relax, enjoy freedom and physical exercise – a combination that helped our mental well-being and kept the team motivated.

Throughout the training, we were subject to the company rules applicable to all employees. In the early 1950s – the period of my early training – we had something called 'Indentured Apprenticeships', which was a contract between parent or guardian and the providing company that guaranteed completion of training. There was a paragraph in the apprenticeship agreement signed by my parents, me and the employer that stated, 'If the Apprentice shall wilfully disobey the lawful orders of the Employer… Or shall grossly misconduct himself, he may, without notice, be discharged from the Company'.

So, any miscreant, for things including sexual misconduct (that we've seen reported in the media a lot in recent years), would have been subject to instant dismissal, full stop. It is interesting to contrast that social attitude with recent 'tolerant' understanding and the blatant disregard for good manners and courtesy.

The training school had an intake of sixteen apprentices, overseen by a foreman who was assisted by two charge hands (senior apprentices reaching the end of their five-year training). Together, they were our instructors from whom we learned metal fabrication, how to rivet together test pieces, and machining skills on centre lathes and milling machines. There was a fly-press to aid bending or piercing aluminium components. In short, we learned basic manufacturing skills.

All work was marked and a league table was put up on the noticeboard at the end of each week. This basic training was for a block of twelve weeks, before we were allocated to a department or workshop to continue our development under the guidance of an older, very experienced person.

This is similar to a houseman working under the guidance of a senior doctor or consultant in the hospital setting, although it is doubtful if the medical profession would welcome the comparison.

The two senior apprentices assisting the permanent foreman were selected by the apprentice supervisor and remained in post for six months before being replaced by two other senior apprentices. It was a 'feather in the cap' to be selected because it meant gaining experience of supervising peers and learning how to maintain the discipline necessary to get the job done – very good experience that I was fortunate to enjoy in the final year of my indentured apprenticeship. Also, it was a great boost to morale; a small signal that you belonged and had value to the company.

Each of us did a minimum of two years on the factory floor plus being moved around the company on a six-month cycle. This gave experience of a drawing office or of commercial work interspersed throughout our training period. This was not all. Westland had a regular population of four hundred apprentices. We were divided into eight houses of fifty, each with a house captain. There were many additional activities in which each house would compete for a shield or cup. These activities included twenty-overs knockout cricket matches, a soccer competition, darts, skittles, indoor rifle shooting, table tennis and lawn tennis. Rugby was not included, maybe because to select fifteen from fifty and to keep them injury-free was asking too much. Anyway, there was a company rugby club that apprentices could join.

Each house captain had a place on the apprentices committee, which organised all the activities mentioned above under the watchful eye of the apprentice supervisor, who acted very much like a good referee (i.e. most of the time, we were not aware of his overall influence). It was part of our development to take responsibility for our actions. The committee had elected officers of chairman, secretary and treasurer, each charged with producing an annual report for all apprentices to scrutinise before and at the annual general meeting of the Apprentice Association.

While insisting we ran things ourselves, the apprentice supervisor and his staff had an important administrative role. They maintained our individual records. These included a confidential report, made by the head of each section we worked in, as we were moved around the company. Our academic progress at the local technical college was also recorded, as we studied for the Ordinary National Certificate (ONC) for three years and the Higher National Certificate (HNC) for a further two years. The company sponsored the top ten from the HNC results each year to go to university to gain a degree in aeronautical engineering. In addition, all aspects of our work, study and contribution to the running of the Apprentice Association was brought together by the supervisor's staff and the top apprentice of the year was put forward for the award of the Managing Director's Cup, provided that the managing director gave his approval after interviewing that person.

The award was presented at the annual dinner attended by a number of the company directors and visiting dignitaries. Invitations were also issued to our counterparts in other companies who ran similar schemes. There were after-dinner speakers, headed by the visiting speaker, usually well known, with replies coming from the apprentice committee officers.

I managed to fit into the overall scheme with some success, being selected to serve as an assistant to the training school foreman. House captain was a position occupied from my third year – Wallace House. Subsequently, I was made honorary secretary of the Apprentice Association. Each house was named after a past aircraft produced by the company. The sport activities were attractive and I made some academic progress, while my conduct reports surprised me. The greatest surprise and pleasure was to win the Managing Director's Cup as the 'Apprentice of the Year, 1956'. The training, fellowship and socialising enjoyed during my apprenticeship, including the chance to make decisions, take responsibility and to speak in public, all from an early age, are things that I have benefited from throughout my life. Thank you, Westland Aircraft Ltd.

This was all very fine and most large organisations at that time had training schemes, but there were some companies among those organisations who objected to losing their fully trained people to smaller employers who had not contributed to the cost of training. The disquiet rumbled on in the 1950s and 1960s, fuelled by the shortage of skills caused by the war years. There was lobbying by some of the far-sighted politicians to address the inequality of the cost of producing a sufficiently skilled workforce to meet the country's need to compete. The result was the Industrial Training Act 1964, which created industry training boards.

These were boards for the respective sectors of commerce and industry. Each had a system of levies and grants. Organisations were obliged to train recruits, for which they were awarded grants paid for by a per capita levy. The levy was obligatory; the grants were for meeting and maintaining good-quality training standards, set and overseen by their respective training board.

The overall scheme was headed by a tripartite of employers, education and trade unions. The training boards were organised into regions and their training officers inspected and worked with the companies within their geographical region. At the outset, boards worked with employers and education to identify and recommend the standard of training and qualifications for entry into their respective sectors. Also, they determined the nature and length of training required.

In the initial years, a good working relationship of acceptance and understanding of the requirements worked well, until the Department of Employment intruded. Inevitably, their intrusion led to the boards – certainly the EITB (Engineering Industry Training Board) becoming 'civil serviced'. Up to that point, the training officers and their managers were people who had experience of working within the industry they served.

Secondary legislation in 1991 saw the EITB absorbed into the Engineering Construction Industry Training Board (ECITB). Previously, the EITB covered manufacturing activities as well as engineering construction. It is tempting to ask, "Why the change?"

In the period up to 2015, the influence – and, maybe, relevance – of the training boards diminished. During that time, they were the subject to a three-year review by the Department for Business, Innovation and Skills. Who thought that one up? It made a final report in December 2015. In October 2016, the government commissioned a review of industrial training boards. Presumably, this was to identify and review what had happened to the remnants of the original concept and operation. Strangely and expensively, we seem to have come full circle. Once again, our government and the media are publishing the value of apprenticeships and, after fifty years, we still have a skills shortage. It is questionable whether we know how many trained people we need at what rate and where, together with a projection of losses due to retirement and natural causes.

The comparison with the history of our NHS is striking. Each worked perfectly well at the outset. Hospitals were run by a secretary and a relatively small administrative staff: a matron, a ward sister, state registered nurses and a proportion of trainee nurses (within their three years of training). Cleaning and catering was under the control of the respective hospitals. Regional hospital boards also had convalescent homes, into which patients were transferred to complete their recovery and so beds became free within the wards. GPs worked out their own shifts to give twenty-four-hour cover.

A health authority and hospital need a vigilant purchasing team, strong enough to challenge the large pharmaceutical companies and other suppliers regarding prices and reliability of delivery and quality (i.e. value for money). Waste should be a forbidden word. Why are sterile sealed packaged items thrown away instead of stored for future use? There are probably other examples, which is worrying.

When health authorities can demonstrate, not simply claim, efficiency, then there is a stronger case for sufficient funds to maintain the NHS. In my memory, no problem was ever solved simply by throwing money at it without accountability.

Those within the NHS do a remarkably good job. Over a similar period of time, training, education and health provision have shared common factors. Those factors are progressive government interference, over-regulation and increased paperwork at the expense of those who know best – the practitioner; regular reorganisation – often on a three-year cycle; and a continuous fight for funding and recognition of the frontline professionals' contribution. One can only wonder why we have not applied basic good management practices. Each successive government, irrespective of party dogma, seems to believe that change and throwing money at the problem of the moment is 'the answer'.

8th June, 1946

To-day, as we celebrate victory, I send this personal message to you and all other boys and girls at school. For you have shared in the hardships and dangers of a total war and you have shared no less in the triumph of the Allied Nations.

I know you will always feel proud to belong to a country which was capable of such supreme effort; proud, too, of parents and elder brothers and sisters who by their courage, endurance and enterprise brought victory. May these qualities be yours as you grow up and join in the common effort to establish among the nations of the world unity and peace.

George R.I.

The letter sent to all schoolchildren by King George VI at the end of World War II.

IMPORTANT WAR DATES

1939
SEP 1. Germany invaded Poland
SEP 3. Great Britain and France declared war on Germany; the B.E.F. began to leave for France
DEC 13. Battle of the River Plate

1940
APR 9. Germany invaded Denmark and Norway
MAY 10. Germany invaded the Low Countries
JUNE 3. Evacuation from Dunkirk completed
JUNE 8. British troops evacuated from Norway
JUNE 11. Italy declared war on Great Britain
JUNE 22. France capitulated
JUNE 29. Germans occupied the Channel Isles
AUG 8–OCT 31. German air offensive against Great Britain (Battle of Britain)
OCT 28. Italy invaded Greece
NOV 11–12. Successful attack on the Italian Fleet in Taranto Harbour.
DEC 9–11. Italian invasion of Egypt defeated at the battle of Sidi Barrani

1941
MAR 11. Lease-Lend Bill passed in U.S.A.
MAR 28. Battle of Cape Matapan
APR 6. Germany invaded Greece
APR 12–DEC 9. The Siege of Tobruk
MAY 20. Formal surrender of remnants of Italian Army in Abyssinia
MAY 20–31. Battle of Crete
MAY 27. German battleship Bismarck sunk
JUNE 22. Germany invaded Russia
AUG 12. Terms of the Atlantic Charter agreed
NOV 18. British offensive launched in the Western Desert
DEC 7. Japanese attacked Pearl Harbour
DEC 8. Great Britain and United States of America declared war on Japan

1942
FEB 15. Fall of Singapore
APR 16. George Cross awarded to Malta
OCT 23–NOV 4. German-Italian army defeated at El Alamein
NOV 8. British and American forces landed in North Africa

1943
JAN 31. The remnants of the 6th German Army surrendered at Stalingrad
MAY   Final victory over the U-Boats in the Atlantic
MAY 13. Axis forces in Tunisia surrendered
JULY 10. Allies invaded Sicily
SEP 3. Allies invaded Italy
SEP 8. Italy capitulated
DEC 26. Scharnhorst sunk off North Cape

1944
JAN 22. Allied troops landed at Anzio
JUNE 4. Rome captured
JUNE 6. Allies landed in Normandy
JUNE 13. Flying-bomb (V.1) attack on Britain started
JUNE   Defeat of Japanese invasion of India
AUG 25. Paris liberated
SEP 3. Brussels liberated
SEP 8. The first rocket-bomb (V.2) fell on England.
SEP 17–26. The Battle of Arnhem
OCT 20. The Americans re-landed in the Philippines

1945
JAN 17. Warsaw liberated
MAR 20. British recaptured Mandalay
MAR 23. British crossed the Rhine
APR 25. Opening of Conference of United Nations at San Francisco
MAY 2. German forces in Italy surrendered
MAY 3. Rangoon recaptured
MAY 5. All the German forces in Holland, N.W. Germany and Denmark surrendered unconditionally
MAY 9. Unconditional surrender of Germany to the Allies ratified in Berlin
JUNE 10. Australian troops landed in Borneo
AUG 6. First atomic bomb dropped on Hiroshima
AUG 8. Russia declared war on Japan
AUG 9. Second atomic bomb dropped on Nagasaki
AUG 14. The Emperor of Japan broadcast the unconditional surrender of his country
SEP 5. British forces re-entered Singapore

MY FAMILY'S WAR RECORD

32

Jackie's Wedding, August 1982; both equally delighted.

Sons, Kevin (L) and Rob (R). My "Two Minders". The background is not a prison wall, it's our house in Portbury, near Bristol.

Mr. D. C. Collins, works director of Westland Aircraft (third from right) with a group of prize-winning apprentices.

The proudest moment of my apprenticeship. Mr Lobb, Apprentice supervisor, is 4th from right.

The Managing Directors' Cup. Apprentice of the year, Westland Aircraft Ltd, 1956

Inscription reads "Achieved at Tickenham G.C on 195yds hole using a 3 iron. 20th May 2000. Registration No. 6500"

10 h.p Wolsley in which I passed my test, in 1951 (first time!)

Mentone', Coombe Lane, Yeovil (mother is standing guard). Lived there until 14 years old.

The Grammar School, Crewkerne

Ready for the off, aged 8, in 1942

My wife, Norma, on holiday with me in Copenhagen, 2019

Holy Trinity Church, Yeovil. Circ 1954. Norma and I were married here on 17 December 1957. The church no longer exists but we were not responsible for its demise!

May 1958. Our very first car – bought for £25 cash. It was an 8 horse power Triumph: side valve engine, manual advance/retard (on steering wheel centre), with four doors that were 'gull wings' giving no central pillar –very handy for loading a carry-cot.

My pal, Paddy. Aged 13 and two months. Sadly he died in the year of this photograph, almost 14 years old and was greatly missed.

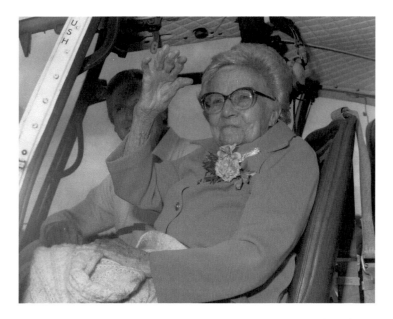

My grandmother, Lottie Martin, on a celebratory flight courtesy of Westland Helicopters Ltd, Yeovil, on her hundredth birthday (1986). It had been her lifetime ambition to ride in a helicopter.

chapter three

The First Job & Beyond

After completing my five-year apprenticeship, I transferred to the drawing office as a junior design draughtsman, which involved technical drawing while standing at a large drawing board that could be angled to a comfortable working position. A senior person guided me and oversaw whatever design talent was possessed at that stage of my career.

Three years later, I transferred to the stress office, where calculations were made to ensure that aircraft components and, indeed the whole aircraft, were of sufficient strength to withstand the loads put upon them as the aircraft performed within its prescribed flight envelope. All calculations were checked by a second person to provide an essential second opinion. My humble role was within the 'check stress' section – a less-demanding task than making initial calculations. This was one of the few occasions in my working life when the numerous formulae and methods of working that had been learned during the technical college education were actually applied.

The local technical college drew its part-time evening teaching staff from the stress office and the aerodynamics department. This was how my experience of teaching first-year Ordinary National Certificate mathematics and engineering drawing was gained. I taught for two years and enjoyed doing it – and the fact that I had to resit some of my exams during my apprenticeship, I believe, made me a better teacher because it gave me an understanding of some students' problems. Sometimes, those who enter teaching as a consequence of their academic brilliance do not make good teachers, because of occasional intolerance of those who experience difficulty in understanding what is being taught. In short, they cannot see a problem. They can be so bright that they jump to answers, missing out a step-by-step, slower explanation. After one particular evening mathematics lesson, the college vice-principal was waiting outside the lecture room. My first thought was 'What have I done now?' To my amazement, he said, "I have been stood outside in the dark watching you. You had them eating out of your hand. Have you thought of teaching full-time? I think you would be good at it."

This literally came out of the dark, if not out of the blue. It set off a whole chain of events culminating in my resignation from Westland Aircraft upon being accepted on a one-year full-time teacher-training course at Garnett College, University of London. There were three establishments offering training for teachers within further education, in Bolton, Wolverhampton and London. I took the plunge and had the privilege of studying full-time for a year, supported by a grant made available because there was a serious shortage of teachers in further education in the 1960s.

We were married with two children at the time and I have my wife, Norma, a state registered nurse, to thank for her support in the risk to our income and the inconvenience of separation. Our home was in a village just outside Yeovil, Somerset. The cost of travelling to and from London was eased by sharing transport with a fellow adult student, linking up en route at his home in Warminster, Wiltshire.

Towards the end of the course, reality hit me. There was no guarantee I would get a teaching post. In which case, I had put myself out of work, with very depleted residual funds. Fortunately, I got a successful interview at North Devon Technical College in Barnstaple. A double bonus was that it was at a grade higher than some people thought possible and in glorious Devon. Much later, it was a surprise to learn from the head of the engineering department that there had been 106 applicants. It was only then I realised how lucky I had been.

The interview panel was a study in human nature: some local dignitaries, a clergyman, a local successful farmer and the principal. One of them had appeared disinterested to the point of nodding off – it was a hot day. When it seemed proceedings were coming to a close, this gentleman jerked himself upright. Now fully alert, he said, "D'you think you'll like it yer?" To which I replied with an emphatic "Yes." Clearly, he had made his choice.

It was a joyous time of teaching maths and engineering science, and overseeing a science laboratory and two drawing offices. Part of the job entailed ordering necessary items for the year on an annual basis. Two strange rituals existed. If your initial interview was successful, you were not allowed to claim travel expenses. If you failed your interview, you could claim expenses. When ordering for your department, if you did not spend the whole budget, it was cut back the following year by the amount you had not spent. With no incentive to save, some staff would purchase some obscure items simply to use up the entire budget. Strange management, which, if it still exists, would go some way towards explaining why education is always asking for more money.

During my time at the technical college, the holidays were used to write the teaching material for the coming academic year, based upon the published curriculum and upon sets of past examination papers. A more enjoyable holiday task was to visit the local factories, companies and the two forces based nearby: RAF Chivenor and REME (Royal Electrical & Mechanical Engineers). I did so upon arrival in the area and maintained contact throughout. It is surprising what teaching aides could be made with the right contacts. This liaison with local business was to later affect my employment direction, as will become clear a little later.

The enjoyment was enhanced by getting involved in activities outside of teaching engineering. Three of us founded a college soccer club and entered it in one of the North Devon leagues. In our second season, the team won the Holford Cup – a knockout competition. We were all very proud of the achievement because, at the outset, we could only sign players that no one else wanted as their first choice. The three of us spent many evenings coaching the players to get the best from those we had.

Running the annual Christmas ball also came my way, following my predecessor's fine efforts. Without seeking it, I was voted to be chairman of the staff association. The annual meeting was always something of a challenge. If you want a meeting where someone, usually when least expected, will voice a point of order, then attend a gathering of teachers.

The annual 'staff versus students' hockey match was another enjoyable event. I had spent seven seasons with the Westland Hockey Club and as an occasional guest player with Yeovil Hockey Club. The Yeovil club at that time had an England international centre-half, Norman Powell, and two Somerset county players in their ranks, so to be an occasional guest player in such company was a rare pleasure.

The Westland Hockey Club went through one season unbeaten in the 1950s. It was a team effort that we were all proud of. I have fond memories of playing in midfield in front of my close ex-school friend, Rex Beable, at right back. We had a very effective playing style; if he ran upfield to attack, I would automatically drop back to cover the space he left. Obvious, really, but we did it instinctively. Today's soccer gurus recommend it as if it is top class. Rex and I remained friends throughout our lives until his death in 2012, having fought a cancer for a number of years. He was a very good friend and I have his last letter to me – written a few weeks before he died – filed away in my 'personal file'. It is a sad loss when a lifelong friend is no longer with us.

While enjoying the teaching experience, particularly the face-to-face aspect, after three years I was becoming frustrated and irritated by the bureaucracy that enveloped the profession – which was often petty and progressively in the way of actually getting things done. It was causing personal unrest.

This unsettled spell was interrupted by a surprise visitor. The college reception called to tell me there was a gentleman at the reception desk who wished to see me. As it was a period of free time, my response was immediate. He was a man, probably aged in his early sixties, cheerful-looking, as indicated by his smiling greeting. However, his words were: "What the hell are you doing wasting your time here?" To which, quite naturally, and somewhat indignantly, I replied, "I beg your pardon!" He then explained himself.

He was from the Engineering Industry Training Board (EITB) and was the senior officer in charge of the Plymouth office. The regional office for the South West was in Bristol. With a twinkle in his eye, he said that people in Devon and Cornwall looked upon Bristol as the edge of the Midlands, hence his office in Plymouth. It was intriguing when he said that an important part of his job was to visit and liaise with all the engineering companies in his patch. He had been doing this in the Barnstaple area, where my name kept being mentioned wherever he went. It was flattering to hear him say that all the comments about me were favourable and that an excellent rapport had been built with the managers of the local firms. The training board was just getting started and was looking for staff. As I had first-hand experience in industry and was now teaching, he thought I had an ideal profile and should write to the regional manager with my CV.

This man would eventually become a good friend, and whose company I enjoyed whenever work brought us together. As progress was made through the ranks, it was necessary to establish a practical and courteous working relationship. Many a joke and a laugh sprinkled our time in the Plymouth area and when the whole team came together for its regular monthly meeting. During one of our meetings at his home, he told of a recent visit to one of the factories in a Cornish fishing town, which typified the relaxed atmosphere adopted by the local factory bosses.

His appointment to meet the managing director of the seaside factory was at 9am. He arrived a little early, as a courtesy, and sat in the director's office, which overlooked the floor of the machine shop, to wait for him. The place remained empty for half an hour before one man appeared and started work on one of the vacant machines. Then another arrived a little while later, then another man, and so it went on until eventually the managing director arrived full of apologies. My colleague told him that he had been sat there for some time before any workers appeared and then they only came as a trickle as the shop filled gradually.

"Yes, I know," said the boss.

"But how can you run a business that way?"

The boss replied, "It's when there be fish in the bay, the men go out in their boats."

"How is it you let them get away with it?"

The boss replied, "There's no problem. Cos they'm my boats they'm be 'iring."

A feature of regular meetings is that they can reach a level of complacency. The boss reports back from London HQ and the regional team listens to a fair amount of detail, which isn't of great consequence and help to our clients. He has achieved briefing us thoroughly; missing out only how many drinks of tea were served and biscuits consumed. We all go our separate ways until the next time. I suspect the civil service operates in a similar fashion. The clue is in the time it takes for good ideas to be acted upon. It's a funny old world.

Five years with the training board was enough for me, as our work became more akin to a roving civil servant than a down-to-earth advisor working with resident training officers to achieve targets of measurable cost–benefit. I had been fortunate to be in a specialist team in the early years, seconded to a succession of companies and practising what the training board preached, and achieving tangible, beneficial results.

Encouraged by the kind comments of these company contacts, I formed my own limited liability company in 1973 and chose a registered name of Welkin Consultants Ltd – a training services company. The chosen registered title accurately described the purpose of the enterprise. Welkin means sky and that seemed a positive direction in which to aim.

The EITB regional office was kind enough to keep occasional contact and to provide a degree of commercial benefit. The early stages went well. However, in the second year, work became spasmodic and courses based at the local Chamber of Commerce became a necessity until a light appeared at the end of the tunnel. The light was that Ford Bridgend contacted me and I travelled from my Bristol office to a meeting with the plant's managing director, with the promise of a large contract that would transform my business. We agreed an outline programme and fee structure. This would be confirmed in writing and a start date agreed. It would entail me calling upon some of my associates, but with the possibility of taking on employees for the first time. In short, a breakthrough was within reach.

On the way home from that successful meeting in Bridgend, the announcement from Prime Minister Edward Heath of a three-day working week came through the car radio. This was his response to the impact of the miners' strikes. For my little company, the timing could not have been worse. The very next morning, the managing director at Bridgend was on the telephone to say, "Sorry, Adrian, I have to cancel our verbal contract. We have no alternative but to look very closely at all our contracts and external services and cut back sharply. I am sorry, it looked very promising, but I hope you understand."

Indeed, I did understand, I faced a worrying vacuum of assignments and also needed to cut back. Two things came to my rescue. The EITB regional manager had offered me my job back, not as a senior training officer but as part of a small consulting team that the board was putting together. The offer was not immediate because things needed to be finalised, but they were finding it difficult to recruit people with commercial experience and I had gone out and got it at the sharp end.

A definite offer was made to me, which I refused, explaining that the salary offered was less than enjoyed recently. A second improved offer was made that was also insufficient, before a third offer that I was glad to accept, knowing there was little choice, taking full account of the situation that existed and knowing there would be little chance of a further offer. There was a depressive mood in the country generally; every organisation in the manufacturing and commercial sectors was tightening their belts and many service companies suffered severe losses.

The second thing that came to my rescue was the fact that company accounts were kept carefully, particularly cash flow. So my decision was as clear as it was disappointing – close the company, which was done via the legal requirements of Companies House. The only thing of questionable value was the client list and goodwill. Both were made *ex gratia* to a business acquaintance, Sadly, contacts are essential, but they are not contracts and, as such, have no tangible value.

The main assignment during my time back with the EITB is the subject of Chapter 4, 'Time Spent in Kuwait'. A complication arose upon my return to the UK. There had been some correspondence with a leading accountancy company regarding the possibility of working in their business consultancy team. This had gone backwards and forwards somewhat vaguely for some months until an offer was received out of the blue. This was accepted because it promised a return to the kind of life enjoyed in the early time as my own boss. The team was known as associates of the accountancy practice and specialised in recruitment, trading and profitability analysis, and feasibility studies, with a clientele of small to medium-sized companies across a wide range of disciplines and throughout the UK.

They wanted me to start as soon as possible. I was catapulted into this new environment by reporting at the

Birmingham headquarters of the consultancy wing. After a brief introduction on day one, the first assignment was at a road building company based in Cheshire. It was to undertake a trading and profitability analysis. It was fortunate that some basic training in financial management had been obtained. This had been at a time when company accountants were having a disproportionate influence over qualified engineers when it came to major operational decisions. Without that background, I would have been completely out of my depth, instead of almost out of my depth. The situation was saved by an accountant colleague joining me, ostensibly to carry out an audit of the company accounts.

I undertook a number of assignments in small or medium-sized organisations across the UK, but there were problems. I was well received by the Bristol office and enjoyed, indeed preferred, working alongside the people there, getting on well with the insolvency head – hardly surprising given my background! I believed that part of my brief was to generate business for the Bristol area and, consequently, I produced an initial annual report of the financial value of work completed and a list of possible prospective clients. This was as I had worked previously and there were some promising signs of further work. Subsequently, however, I was made aware that, in some people's eyes, I had worked outside and beyond my brief. Unfortunately, I learned this after I had left the consultancy, having reacted precociously to a poor annual performance assessment, thereby putting myself out of a job. I'll explain this a little more later.

In this kind of work, it was difficult to reconcile actual

achievement for the client because of the high daily fee. They could ill afford that additional burden. It was because they were not making profit or just not getting anywhere with their business that we were involved – often at the behest of their bank.

An idea put to the consultancy board was that instead of leaving the client with a report and walking away, why not work collaboratively? I suggested that we lower the fee and work alongside an appointed senior employee of the client, implementing our bright ideas to the point that it became self-sustaining. We could write a report in a 'carry on' handbook style and retire from the scene, having made a significant impact upon the efficiency and morale of that client. To the best of my knowledge, the idea never saw the light of day.

On reflection, no induction training was received and I neither fitted the organisation nor reached the standard expected of me. This mismatch came to a head at a personal review meeting. The managing director suggested I should look for another job. In surprise, disgust and anger, I walked out, never to return. This was the end of a valuable experience in the world of small businesses, for which I retained great respect and remained in casual contact with some of them. The report produced for clients had to comply with a standardised content, killing the element of broad thinking, style and content that fitted the individual characteristics of the client's situation. This was frustrating and restrictive.

So, at the age of forty-five, I was out of work for the second time in my life (there was a brief gap between winding up my business and rejoining the EITB).

Arrogantly, I assumed that as a chartered engineer and membership of three different professional institutions, I would soon find employment. Until this point, working life had been a progressive success, I had never been 'asked' to look for another job and this was my own fault. I should have ticked over at the consultancy until finding another job. To be out of work was a drastically new experience and a shock.

Thanks to a good friend, I joined a life insurance company as an agent on commission, i.e. nil basic salary. Absolute disaster! There was too much empathy with potential investors, particularly regarding pension schemes. The empathy too often grew to sympathy, resulting in too few sales being closed. I hated cold-calling, which I saw as intruding into people's lives uninvited. It got to a point where resignation from that type of work saved my sanity and health – it was beginning to depress me. It was very unsettling and never to be repeated.

One day, I was sat at home feeling sorry for myself. It was a time when Lord Tebbit (then Norman Tebbit MP) said that anyone out of work should stop moaning, get on their bike and look for work. So, maybe, the mood of the nation got to me. I took the advice literally. We lived in an area of Somerset that had an industrial estate of small businesses. It was a couple of miles from home. It was a fine day, so I walked to the estate. The opportunity of walking in the fresh air would lift my spirits.

There were twenty-two units in the industrial estate and I knocked on the door of each one in turn, explaining I was looking for work – any type of work – because I refused to live off the state. Meanwhile, I got twenty-one refusals and approached the last one with some misgiving. It was a deep-freeze warehouse. They said that the only vacancy they could offer was a labourer in their deep-freeze area as someone had left the previous week. The hours were 8am to 5.30pm (Monday to Friday) and maybe the occasional Saturday morning. I cannot recall the wage, but it was way below the minimum wage of the present day. I took it; it was a morale boost. Life was teaching me that, when unemployed, you should not confine the search for work with the desire to match the status of previous jobs. Take what is offered as a stepping-stone to recovering your situation.

Thick, warm clothing was supplied, together with lined boots and a warm, woolly hat, so that I now looked the part. We worked all day in $-22°$ packing items listed on an order sheet into cardboard boxes, sealing them and then carrying them to the loading bay, ready for colleagues to load onto the large delivery lorries. Arriving on the first morning, having parked my bike, I was welcomed with the news that: "The last bloke, a youngster, packed it in after a fortnight – he couldn't stand the pace". Hoping they would not ask my age, I introduced myself and got on with the job. No induction training here; just get stuck in.

In one sense, it was a repeat of my time working in Yeovil Town Council's landscape gardening department during a university vacation. Remember, it was as a mature student that teacher training was done. I was an adult addition to an existing work gang. However, because of genuine effort being applied and a good day's work being done, the full-timers soon accepted me as one of them.

The thing that was noticeable in both situations was that

when you work with people content with their lot and not driven to achieve any kind of promotion, you get the genuine person – cooperative, sharing, joking etc. In 'the freezer' was a similar team of people; cheerful and happy to muck in and help each other. This atmosphere and team spirit went a long way to restoring my confidence and morale. I was working again at a level that sharpened an appreciation of what really matters when it is 'backs to the wall'.

Here is where the love, support and work of my wife must be recognised. Norma qualified as a state registered nurse and worked as a staff nurse at Bristol and Yeovil hospitals before marriage and three children. When the children reached the age of 'middle school', she worked as a receptionist at a local general medical practice in an area of Bristol. The practice would only employ qualified ex-nurses as receptionists, thus striking a balance between initial clarity of patients' needs and acting as a 'gatekeeper' to ease the path of the patient to their doctor.

Norma reached a stage of wishing to progress when the children were of an age to make it possible. She embarked upon a course of study at a well-known organisation over a four-year period and qualified as a remedial massage therapist. Later, she progressed via further training and qualified as an osteopath, before establishing a private practice in osteopathy and remedial massage. The private practice came much later. At the time of my self-inflicted demise, she was at the remedial massage stage, so we had income and she retained her small car for domiciliary work. I had had to sell my car and return to cycling, using our eldest son's bicycle. It became a vehicle for fitness as well as transport and was a positive part of a difficult time.

During the time of turning my back on the professional consultancy company, trying to sell insurance policies for a large, well-known insurance company, working in a freezer warehouse and cycling instead of motoring, I continued studying for a Master's degree as a mature external (part-time) student at the University of Bath. I had started the degree for two reasons: I was bored with the EITB scene at the time, and the sickness that had interrupted sitting the latest edition of a school certificate had, perhaps, sat in my subconscious as unfinished business. There was now a determination to finish the job.

The university tutor was amazed that I dealt with one of my job changes without disrupting my studies to achieve an MSC (Management), which majored in organisation and psychology. On a lighter note, I qualified in the same month as our eldest grandson was born. Not many people can say that or, indeed, would wish to make the same frivolous claim.

The content and overall experience helped during my time at Rolls Royce Ltd and certainly at the doctor's practice in Somerset. Because of team-leading the complementary practitioners – this evolved with time – I also chaired several meetings during the research by the practice in conjunction with Exeter University. In that environment of medical doctors, university professors and complementary therapists, there was evidence of various differing professional viewpoints and personalities at play. So, it was not all theory but relevant to life itself.

It was while cycling home one early spring evening that the lowest point of despair came over me. What an impetuous fool I had been. I had no car, no worthwhile income and nothing of any consequence in sight. Progressive career advancement had crashed at a time of peak earning ability. It was a time of utter despair and I could not see a way forward.

It was at about this time that my wife and I attended a play by an amateur dramatics group. It was excellent and made a welcome break from our current situation. After the performance, we met an ex-colleague from the EITB team. After the usual pleasantries, he said that Rolls Royce were looking for a training manager and he thought I should apply.

That man will never know the part he played in the process of turning my life around. I wrote to the personnel director with my CV. The training manager post had been filled by an internal appointment of someone with little experience of training. However, there was a job as a training officer, which I accepted. The recovery was now possible, but not without a few hiccups.

While very grateful to be in full-time employment again, particularly with such a well-known organisation as Rolls Royce Ltd aero engines, humble pie was on the menu. It meant stepping back to the level and type of work I had done fifteen years previously and, inwardly, it was hard to accept the step back. Fortunately, over a five-year period, progress was made to a senior management level upon being made management training and development manager for two of the national business groups. There were five autonomous groups formed because of a major reorganisation designed to focus more clearly upon the technical and financial performance of the company.

Coming from a commercial and consultancy

background, it was very noticeable from the outset that there was a general lack of appreciation of the commercial value of the very high technical engineering operations. There was little mention of financial topics.

A one-day course was designed, 'Finance without Mystery', in which I led the attendees in forming a fictional business to the stage of applying some standard ratios that measure the financial health of a trading company. Deliberately, I had included the case of their own company that had been bailed out by the government some years ago. The surprise upon the faces of those senior managers when they were told they had just identified the failure of their own company was a sight to behold. They had been able to calculate the weakness that led to the previous problems and to question why their predecessors had not seen it for themselves. In a sense, the managers of that fateful era had been obsessed with collective technological cleverness and had been blind to the worrying financial clues that were evident. A series of these courses was run in an attempt to spread awareness of the financial consequences of managerial decisions.

This was a time of launching some serious reductions in the total number of employees. A team comprising the corporate personnel director, the corporate training manager and myself was formed and we toured the company sites explaining the procedure of the reduction programme and the measures to be taken to minimise the impact for the employees affected. It was organised alongside five-day retirement courses run at various sites across the country. These covered such topics as financial planning (by invited professional financial advisors), how to stay fit and active, part-time jobs and voluntary work etc.

The job involved frequent travel from the Bristol office of Rolls Royce to its other sites around Britain. One trip in particular stands out. It was the return flight from the site in East Kilbride, involving a flight from Glasgow to East Midlands Airport. It was an eventful journey.

Alongside two company directors, we would be departing Glasgow Airport in winter darkness, with a very strong westerly wind blowing across the runway. Even as it stood ready to roll, the wind was sufficient to rock the wings of the British Airways short-haul aircraft.

We departed on time and upon lift-off, the pilot instructed us to keep our seat belts on throughout the journey and to expect turbulence, which happened continuously. The rocking and dipping motion began to affect me and nausea soon overtook me. I managed to deal with it until we hit an almighty pocket; the aircraft dropped as if it was a hotel lift in free fall; the overhead covers burst open and showered all the passengers with assorted cases, briefcases and loose bags. It was momentarily frightening and too much for my stomach, which spilt its contents into the paper bag in front of me. This was very disappointing and ruined my aim to last until we landed at East Midlands Airport.

Once landed, my colleagues and I went our separate ways – to the Derby area or, in my case, by car to go home to Portbury, a village outside Bristol. Because I felt unwell and despite the night chill, the car windows were kept down to enjoy the fresh air. It was the only time that recovery was not achieved by the end of a journey home, which lasted about an hour and a half. On reflection, some years later, it was surprising that our aircraft was allowed to take off in such severe night conditions and maybe we had all had a lucky escape in surviving the sudden big vertical drop mid-flight.

This involvement was an opportunity to consider voluntary redundancy for myself, but not before making good provision via an additional qualification that would take me away from manufacturing and commerce. Strangely, this was forced upon me in a way that was a very serious surprise.

At home, it was a sunny Sunday and we had enjoyed a good lunch. I was relaxing in a chair and managing to stay awake. Outside was the front garden in which the season's tulips had died back and the tops needed clearing away. With my shadow, Paddy the Labrador, I went out to clear the flower border. As I bent to move the dead leaves, they became a little blurred, so I bent a little closer. Suddenly, everything went blank. I recovered consciousness, to find myself stretched out on the settee in the lounge and looking at the local doctor on duty. Over his shoulder, I caught sight of the ambulance that had reversed down the drive and was parked by the front door of the house, ready to provide me with a free ride courtesy of the NHS.

Fortunately, the ambulance was not required to take me into hospital and I was told to rest where I was. My own doctor visited the following morning and repeated the need to rest, saying it seemed that I had 'fitted' – a term that I objected strongly to.

Paddy the dog had attracted the immediate attention of our neighbours by barking furiously while standing by me.

Our neighbour and Norma rushed out. Norma applied appropriate first aid because she thought I may have had a stroke and neighbours who had joined her by this time carried me indoors.

Over the following days, various tests were done. Thankfully, there was no trace of a heart attack and three weeks of complete rest were ordered. This was just as well because I had no energy whatsoever; it was as if it had been switched off or that a fuse had blown. It was during this enforced rest that I read an advertisement that read: 'Why not train as a chiropodist?' Now, I had said on a number of occasions, usually when we were returning from a medical conference, how I wished I could have done medical training, to which my wife replied, "Why don't you? What's stopping you?" The answer was "Nothing" and the advertisement in front of me was part of the answer.

I wish to break off here to acknowledge the love, encouragement and due credit to my wife, Norma, throughout my varied life. When our three children reached secondary school age, she helped at a nearby infant school before taking a post as a receptionist at the local GP practice. The GP surgery only employed state registered nurses on reception so that each receptionist was able to clarify the needs of patients over the phone, as a preliminary to the doctor's consultation.

She became very interested in physical therapies and began regular travel to Blackpool and other cities to attend training in Swedish massage initially, then manipulative therapy, which led on to her qualifying as an osteopath. It was during these busy times, while Norma was studying, that our children became a great support, not least in practising their cooking skills! Over the following years, she established a private practice that developed the manipulative aspects of her work with loyal clients.

Returning to the defining event in my life, the collapse in the garden was a very strange experience. In my teens, there had been a couple of fainting episodes that were part of my growing at a fast rate. The recovery from a brief faint was relatively quick and life just continued, but this was very different. It was a ten-minute vacuum within my life. Temporary confusion preceded the full recovery of consciousness. Some years later, I asked a friend who had survived a car crash what he could remember of the incident. He said he had no recollection – it was a blank. It seemed that our respective 'blanks' were very similar. Maybe, it is the body's ability to blank these incidents from our memory and, in so doing, aid recovery.

Ever curious, I researched how and why I had collapsed because the medical profession could not explain it. There was no trace of heart attack and no further episode, but I read about some research done in Italy on similar episodes that left no clue to the cause. Their finding was that it was a break in the electrical signal from the brain to the heart. A break in that system can cause the symptoms I suffered and leaves no measurable trace. Clearly, if the signal had not returned to normal sufficiently quickly, I would not be writing this personal account and death would have happened at the age of fifty-two.

The forced rest provided a chance to ponder the kind of life I was leading. Work had been at an ever-increasing rate, driving or flying between the company's factories around the UK. Nature had taken a hand and applied a semicolon to the flow of events. It was time to take charge of my life and not allow it to run me.

Even Paddy, my Labrador shadow, changed his behaviour from 'harem scarum' to calm behaviour. It seemed that his instinct led him to behave differently. Any owner of a young male Labrador would tell you that they are prone to charge off into the distance to follow a scent. No amount of calling or whistling would have the slightest effect, yet when we went on our first walk, after four weeks, he would only go a short distance before stopping and waiting for me to catch up at a very slow pace. At the early stage of my recovery, I had little physical energy and walking was at an unusually leisurely pace. He was an amazing companion and I was proud of him and his intelligence. Years later, in 1990, when he died, I cried. The best and most loyal dog I ever had.

It was a wonder that the children took all of this in their stride, with no apparent mental bruising. We can be grateful for the combined successful outcome.

Strangely, Norma and I had a twenty-year spell when we seemed to take it in turns to be absent from the home, with me travelling a great deal in the same period that Norma was travelling to study, to do advanced work and to attend various conferences to keep up to date with the advancing techniques. It was my attendance as a guest as these conferences that rekindled my lifelong interest in health and the outcome is sprinkled throughout this book.

During the enforced rest period, I applied and was accepted at a well-known establishment near London that offered the opportunity to learn chiropody by distance learning. This was my introduction to anatomy and physiology. There followed residential weekends, some evening lectures and summer holidays spent doing the surgical aspects, under constant tutelage, on volunteer members of the public, free of charge. It was a thorough training over three years that proved invaluable. It was only after I qualified that I learnt the pass mark for the theory paper was eighty per cent. This high level was a deliberate policy to ensure all graduates were well qualified and able to treat patients safely and with confidence.

I encountered some scepticism and a somewhat dismissive attitude to this pattern of education and training. Yet, in practice, there were few shortcomings and the number of patients increased by word of mouth. The college provided a unique chance for those who realised later in life that they had chosen the wrong career path. It provided me with the chance to make a significant change by acquiring a recognised professional qualification and gaining the opportunity to help patients. In many respects, the training was very similar to that provided by the Open University, particularly the opportunity to learn while remaining employed.

Before launching into a way of life away from industry, training, commerce and consultancy, the lessons learned when in private business were now put to good use. Instead of borrowing to set up business, the banks would and could be avoided. Personal income was sufficient to purchase equipment of a patient's treatment chair, a medical cabinet, a surgical drill, a portable surgical grinder, a swivel chair for me and essential sterilising equipment. A private practice was being built in the evenings and, on Saturday mornings, while retaining my day job. This was helped further by a reduction in the work at the company. Others above and around me had been shocked into realising that, perhaps, too much had been expected of me. The change in the attitude of colleagues and seniors towards me was a great surprise. On the return to work, I was almost allowed to freewheel.

It was fortunate that this pre-planning coincided with the launch of the company's fair redundancy packages. This would present an opportunity for me. It depended upon a balance being negotiated and the timing of any deal. The balance was how to let the company know that an offer might be acceptable without putting myself out of a job prematurely. The earlier impetuous action of 'pressing the ejector seat button' from the accountancy consultancy team would not be repeated.

The personnel director was approached and a confidential meeting arranged. It was put to him that redundancy might be considered if and when the terms were known. As a safeguard against my view being known too widely, I said, "By the way, if this goes wrong, I will be back to see you." In large organisations, it can be difficult to gauge where genuine loyalties and self-interest exist. Thankfully, the safeguard proved unnecessary. A very fair offer was made that was accepted. I was already for take-off, with grateful thanks to the personnel director and colleagues for their integrity and kind help.

This is a suitable time to point out that I resigned all my professional engineering-based qualifications. These comprised the status as a chartered engineer for which the qualification was corporate membership of one or more of the institutions that formed the Council of Engineering

Institutions. I had two: member of the Institution of Mechanical Engineers (IMechE) and member of the Royal Aeronautical Society (RAeS). This was in addition to membership of the Institute of Management Consultants (IMC) and membership of the British Institute of Management (BIM).

The reason was simple: if I had retained them, there would have been the temptation of 'Well. if it doesn't work out, there is always the industrial/commercial world to fall back on'. If that prop was removed, my new life had to succeed. It was a self-inflicted huge incentive.

This included a completely fresh study of anatomy, physiology, pathology and chiropody practice, and the need to ensure I qualified in my new professional life. So, qualification in chiropody was obtained, as mentioned elsewhere, professional indemnity insurance was taken out and the decks were cleared for a completely new way of life.

The domiciliary chiropody continued in the evenings and Saturdays before an established practice was purchased, after seeing the audited accounts covering the past three years of trading. As we had a five-bedroom, detached house, it was possible to practice from home, plus visits. One of the bedrooms was converted to a treatment room and was fully equipped. The patient numbers increased steadily. The bulk of the work was the removal of corns, verrucae and hard skin, nail cutting and filing, with in-growing toenails sometimes presenting a challenge. The college taught an excellent way of removing a wedge of nail, which avoided the nail having to be removed in the vast number of cases, much to the relief of the patient.

The most common skin problem was athlete's foot

(*tinea pedis*). The school advocated bathing the foot in a solution of potassium permanganate crystals. Any suitable bowl will suffice in which to soak the feet for approximately ten minutes. This can be repeated as frequently as recommended by a qualified practitioner. This is an old remedy, used in World War I, where it was known as 'pinky' – the colour of the solution. The soldiers suffered 'trench foot' – a condition caused by having to stand in flooded trenches. The treatment is simple but not known by many doctors or other members of the healthcare fraternity today. The publicity generated by the manufacturers of a variety of foot and hand creams has won the day.

One of my wife's patients had had a fingernail discolouration for years. Nothing seemed to overcome the problem. The 'pinky' approach was suggested and the outcome amazed her. Sometime later, she showed my wife a clear, healthy fingernail. Do not dismiss history – some old ways are valuable and often so simple that some medical scientists are prone to dismiss them out of hand.

During my time spent as a chiropodist, there was a groundswell of magazine articles and a small number of paperbacks about various foot conditions and the importance of the feet to our general health. This focus moved gradually to news about reflexology and I began to get an increasing number of patients asking me about the therapy. This led me to find out about reflexology. The more I read about it, the more interested I became. Here was a hands-on technique that affected the whole body, not just the feet. If I was going to qualify as a therapist and use it as an adjunct to chiropody, it was essential to find a respected organisation in which to learn and also that required its students to qualify via a written examination and practical assessment.

The International Institute of Reflexology (IIR) was my choice. This organisation is one of the oldest reflexology teaching organisations in the western world and is truly international. At the time of my association, it had licensed registered tutors in seven countries throughout the world.

The founder of the institute was Eunice D. Ingham, who was recognised in the western world as the pioneer of reflexology, using the Ingham Method of Reflexology – a patented method closely guarded by the institute. Eunice practised her foot and hand techniques tirelessly throughout the 1930s in the USA, often in an environment of criticism and opposition from the established medical profession. She was still teaching the technique at the age of eighty and died five years later on 10th December 1974.

Her nephew, Dwight Byers (ex-US Army Medical Corp), worked alongside his aunt and eventually took over as head of the institute to continue and spread the teaching and the practise of reflexology, and to build upon over eighty years of research. His book, *Better Health with Foot Reflexology – The Ingham Method*, is, without doubt, a complete and authoritative reference of the therapy. Sadly, Dwight Byers died on 29th August 2020 and I am honoured to record this late tribute to him. He was past President of the IIR and was the most knowledgeable teacher and practitioner of reflexology one could ever meet. He was fun to be with, and a natural guide and inspiration.

Qualifying with an established and respected school was very satisfying and led to the therapy being offered alongside the chiropody. We now had a valuable practice in which my wife offered massage and osteopathic techniques alongside my reflexology and chiropody. It grew entirely by personal recommendation – a happy way to progress.

A point was reached where reflexology work was beginning to outnumber chiropody and a decision needed to be made. It was necessary to decide which speciality to follow and it involved some risk. Would reflexology be able to fill the gap left by dropping chiropody? The decision was the result of circumstance because, out of the blue, a person approached me to see if I would be willing to sell the chiropody practice as a going concern. After due consideration, an agreement was reached, together with an after-sale handover process, over a fixed period of time. Inevitably, there was a drop in income, but within a year the gap had been filled. After a further year, Tony Porter, the UK Director for the IIR, invited me to join his teaching team as a regional director for the South West.

Fortune smiled upon me again when a qualified reflexology colleague moved home from Sussex to Somerset and joined our teaching team. She organised and ran teaching modules at suitable venues across the region. I will always be grateful to Hildergard Edwards for tactfully applying the brakes when my enthusiasm threatened to distort the purpose of a lecture. She became a valued friend and confidant. Equally, I am pleased to count Tony Porter as a long-term friend and fountain of knowledge. He worked all over the world alongside Dwight Byers and I had the good fortune to work with him on numerous teaching modules, seminars and conferences.

When Tony Porter became so busy with his personal work as a writer, teacher and practitioner, which took him all over the world, he resigned as director to concentrate upon those interests. A somewhat eventful and unusual period of time followed for the IIR UK. This was to be expected when someone of Tony's reputation and standing resigns. After a while, Dwight Byers asked if I would consider overseeing the UK operation of the institute, reporting to him directly. This needed some thought because the invitation had come a little late in my working life. Nevertheless, I was pleased to accept and would do my best. This was where it proved useful to have had some business experience. It is surprising how often experience gained previously finds a place in an entirely different situation. It was possible to see the steps that could be taken to restore the UK set-up to the stable condition it deserved.

There was a private meeting with Mr Byers in which we pooled information and ideas and clarified the way ahead. Consequently, regional directors were set up for the North, the Midlands, London, the South East and the West, with the Republic of Ireland and its director as an autonomous entity reporting directly to the President (Dwight Byers). In addition, a number of us joined forces in updating the teaching syllabus and standardising it so that wherever a student was taught, the general theme and stages would be simultaneous and common to all regions.

It is important to emphasise that while the teaching material was to be common across the UK, it would be a framework within which each tutor could enjoy the freedom to deliver the material in their own individual style. We needed to achieve only sufficient control from the centre for a coherent operation and to avoid blunting initiative and affecting morale.

The therapy is often portrayed by the media as a relaxing, light, general massage of the feet and hands. Instead, firm pressure is applied with the tip of the thumb and forefinger or, in advanced form, the knuckle of the thumb or finger are used. The purpose is to treat the whole of the foot or hand and, in the process, find specific tender areas that indicate an imbalance in the patients well-being. A reflexologist does not identify any specific medical condition – that is the prerogative of a medical physician. However, there is a vast amount of anecdotal evidence in support of the treatments helping the body to achieve a balanced state (i.e. homoeostasis).

Reflexologists do not treat specific conditions nor claim to be able to diagnose them, and they do not prescribe medication. These were and remain absolute rules emphasised during training and applied in practice.

There was a report published in *The Times* that highlighted reflexologists' inability to diagnose medical conditions. This was while I was UK Vice President of the IIR and, as such, I wrote a letter to *The Times* correcting the false claim and emphasising that it was an absolute rule that qualified reflexologists were never permitted to diagnose. My response never saw the light of day. I wonder why? It was very unfortunate that the article appeared at a time when there was a coming together of representatives from a number of reflexology societies to form the Reflexology Research Trust. It was independent of any particular institute, society or school, with the prime aim of making the therapy widely acceptable to the public and the medical profession via rigorous research and publication of worthwhile results.

The trust was chaired by an experienced medical physician and latterly full-time research fellow at the Department of Complementary Medicine at the University of Exeter. He was supported by founding members and directors from three different UK reflexology organisations and one well-known, leading reflexologist with long experience of working in the UK and of teaching overseas in numerous countries.

A number of existing research papers were reviewed from Sweden, China and the Far East. Our chairman was somewhat disdainful of them as being insufficiently rigorous. This attitude tended to become a little tiresome. It seemed only work done by reputable UK universities was worthy of recognition. We reached a point where *The Times* article and the failure to publish the IIR response was too much for our most experienced and knowledgeable trustee and he resigned. I followed him a little while later.

Strangely, while the break-up of the research trust was a disappointment, other events were beginning to demand my attention, beyond and in addition to the absorbing work with patients. For example, the king's study into complementary therapies and the effort to get approval of them, leading to their integration within general healthcare. This work was given impetus by the active interest of the then HRH Prince of Wales (now King Charles III).

Things were developing in another area of health in parallel to the king's study. There was a growing momentum for a single, comprehensive qualification for complementary therapists. A number of organisations got together to explore and design such training and qualification. We met in London, bringing together therapies such as reflexology, acupuncture, reiki, Bowen therapy (founded in Australia) and remedial massage etc. The target was to have an improved working association among the therapies with an umbrella national qualification that would unify us and have the acceptance and respect of the established medical world.

In July 1999, soon after I had handed over the coordination of the UK division of the IIR, a letter was received from the Department of Trade and Industry, Companies Administration. This added to the work described in the previous two paragraphs and caused a temporary diversion. Under the Companies Act 1985 and the Business Names Act 1985, the Department was expressing concern that our title included the word 'international' and challenged its validity.

In response, and acting as immediate past Vice President of the IIR (UK), I set out six bullet points, including the work being done in Bosnia, France and Malta, and the fact that the headquarters were in Florida, USA. The institute was international in operation and character and, more to the point, the title had existed by custom and practice some thirty-three years before the Business Names Act 1985 came into being. Consequently, the recent and late misgivings were hard to understand. Our explanation was concluded with the following comment: 'We are confident that the Department will be able to accommodate the genuine desire of the Institute to reflect the international nature of its teaching and, in so doing, continue the Department's effort to help UK enterprises succeed, both at home and overseas.'

Nothing further was heard from the department.

There were significant threats from wider afield. The 'Eurocrats' in Brussels were in the process of issuing yet another directive. This one was the Traditional Herbal Medicine Directive and the Food Supplements Directive. This threatened the freedom of the producers of these products by proposing such demands as to make the cost of researching and producing them prohibitive to all but the multinational pharmaceutical companies.

Once again, action on our behalf was essential and I wrote letters to my local MP, Dr Liam Fox, and to the Right Hon. Earl of Stockton, our 'local' member of the European Parliament at his business address, emphasising the threat to vitamins and minerals. The directive contained a list of allowed food supplements but excluded three hundred safe and popular nutrients on the UK market. In addition, to get a licence under this directive, a product would have to have been in existence in the market for thirty years (including fifteen years in Europe). This was in the early part of 2002, so this meant from 1972 and 1987, respectively. New herbal remedies, or remedies that contained vitamins and/ or minerals, would therefore be banned.

While no response was received from the earl, Dr Fox was very supportive. He sent a comprehensive letter setting out the facts and, together with his colleague, the Shadow Secretary for Health, tabled an Early Day Motion (911). This called on the government to make vigorous efforts to obtain changes to the proposals to protect consumer choice and the livelihood of many hundreds of health-food producers and retailers.

I believe the efforts of the multitude of all concerned, professionals and patients, was the reason concessions were obtained. We are familiar now with recommended daily allowance (RDA) and many products are classified as food products. In essence, it was an attempt to impose the German and French systems of regulating food supplements, herbal and homeopathic products throughout the EU. In both countries, such products are available only on prescription. There were occasions when the EU bureaucracy behaved not as a union of over twenty countries for the common good, but as a collective imposition upon and frustration for farming, fisheries, small and medium-sized business, food distribution, retail and organisers of major events.

These political events illustrate the reality of running any enterprise. Certain events occur that are beyond our control, yet we have to operate within them while safeguarding our business. It is another example of that which overtook my grandad's business, as described.

It might appear strange to include the pros and cons of running a business in the training of reflexologists for membership to the International Institute of Reflexology (IIR). However, in a private practice, there is the need to be a Jekyll and Hyde in the sense that, on one hand, a practitioner needs good business sense and, on the other hand, they must apply the therapy with sympathy and respect for patients – a hard/soft approach.

There was an understandable tendency for students to concentrate solely on the techniques and theory. We would reinforce the need to keep an eye on the finances, too, stressing that there is no point in being a brilliant reflexologist if you allow yourself to go out of business.

Time always seemed to be in short supply, largely due

to the additional duties and responsibilities that came my way. The practice was the core of the work and how fortunate to meet and help such a variety of patients. For over three years in the late 1990s, there was the added bonus of being accepted to work alongside four general medical practitioners at their Warwick House Practice in Taunton, Somerset. It enveloped a masseuse, two osteopaths (one lady, one man), an acupuncturist, a homeopath, a chiropodist, a speech therapist and a reflexologist, each working one day per week. There were monthly practice meetings, alternating between business topics and consideration of conditions causing problems. At these meetings we would each have an opportunity to pool ideas.

At the time, the practice was unique and was instigated by the far-sighted and energetic senior partner Dr Brian Dodson ("Doddy" to his close or long-standing friends). There were magazine articles featuring the exploits of the practice and, on one occasion, Brian and I gave a dual presentation and question-and-answer session at a conference held in the Queen Elizabeth Conference Centre in Westminster, opposite the Houses of Parliament. The audience was large and the event was invigorating.

During my time at Warwick House, a female patient came for reflexology to see if it might help her intolerance to fatty/sweet food. On the fourth visit, she bounded into my room while simultaneously announcing, "I had a cream doughnut, one of my favourites, last week and I was fine. Thank you." The celebration took much of the early part of treatment. This was a further example of there being a third treatment rule. For some reason and for some patients, any tangible benefit from the treatment would manifest itself from the third treatment, given at one a week. It is a pleasure to report that my doughnut patient enjoyed her fat, sweets and snacks from that moment. We must hope that she was able to control her weight.

At my home practice, I met a patient who was a retired prominent cyclist with the well-known Manchester Wheelers. This was relevant and noted because his attitude was one of determination – typical of top sportspeople. His problem was one of recurring cramp that affected his feet and legs, which was hampering the amount of exercise he still enjoyed. From the outset, we agreed I would treat him as many times as it took to achieve improvement that was satisfactory to him and when we reached that point, treatment would stop. In this way, we ensured he would not pay unnecessary fees. Sure enough, after four or five treatments (I cannot remember the exact number as his notes were destroyed, along with all other patient notes, upon my retirement), he said that while he was delighted with the progress made, he thought that was as good as it was going to get.

A number of serving nurses were patients and one lady asked me if I would treat her terminally ill husband, who had cancer. The answer was "Yes", but I explained there would be obvious limitations to any improvement, which, sadly, might be temporary. With those terms accepted, the bed-ridden patient was treated in his own home. The first thing that amazed me was the large number of different tablets prescribed and taken as a daily routine; the whole collection filled a large round biscuit tin of the size that could be a Christmas present. The second thing was his cheerfulness. On the third visit, he said he wanted me to continue treatment because he was feeling a little better.

It was indeed a sad day, when soon after that request, a telephone call was received to tell me that he had died peacefully. I did not see his widow for some months. When she had organised her life sufficiently and was able to talk about her husband, she came to see me. During treatment and some discussion about her late husband, she said, out of the blue, "You know you helped him a great deal and the thing he appreciated above all else was that you gave him back control of his bladder." What a good thing to be told. It lifted my spirits for the remainder of that day, together with a humble feeling that such a small change had meant so much.

There were some very cheerful sessions. One was with a lady who had treatment on a monthly basis. During one morning appointment, we fell into conversation about our elderly nearest and dearest; her father had been staying at their house and had to visit the toilet in the night. Unfortunately, being unfamiliar with the geography and half asleep, he took a wrong turning and urinated down the stairs. We were beside ourselves with laughter as we imagined a ridiculous scene of an illuminated waterfall – a positive outlook upon the mishap. Treatment stopped while we recovered our composure and I recalled a somewhat similar experience with my dear mother, which did not involve a staircase but an unusual receptacle.

There were other times when maintaining a professional manner was put to the test. One very attractive young lady always insisted on removing her jeans, as she found it much easier to relax. A towel was used to keep her dignity and control my blood pressure. Every occupation has its perks.

Sufficient to say that life was busy and very enjoyable in the period of private practice, working with the doctors' practice in Somerset, teaching reflexology, running the UK division of the International Institute of Reflexology, publishing their half-yearly magazine *Ingham International* and maintaining the various accounts related to those activities.

During this busy period, the opportunity arose to study, train and qualify as a Bowen therapist, a practice that originated from the work of Tom Bowen at Geelong, Victoria, Australia. In 1974, Tom Bowen invited a qualified osteopath, Oswald Rentsch, and his wife, Elaine, to study with him. He had no manual, notes or charts and he agreed for them to observe, practice and document his techniques, so that they could preserve the technique in its original form and teach others around the world. To do this, they formed the Bowen Therapy Academy of Australia in 1987, naming it Bowtech (the Bowen technique). When they came to the UK, my wife and I were lucky to be among the first to qualify as a MBTAA – Member of the Bowen Therapy Academy of Australia.

The therapy uses a series of precise moves on soft tissue on specific locations on the body. The moves are light touch and can be done through light clothing, if necessary.

During my time as a practitioner and during subsequent retirement, I have observed the therapy become established worldwide and particularly in America and Europe.

To the uninitiated, the technique appears too simple and gentle to have a real effect, but some results amazed me. There was one occasion in particular. My wife was recovering from surgery and we had made it known that while osteopathic treatment was not available temporarily, Bowen therapy would continue to be offered.

It was during this period that a call was received from a man in agony and desperate to receive relief. He was an existing patient of my wife and so it was explained that Bowen therapy was an alternative opportunity and, really out of desperation, he came to see me. He could only just get up the stairs on hands and knees. My inner thoughts had to remain unexpressed. The situation looked beyond osteopathy and, maybe, would require referral to a specialist surgeon. However, the gentleman agreed to give Bowen therapy a try and stated he did not mind what I did if it would give him relief from pain. This was expressed as colourfully as his dilemma merited.

When he returned in one week, I was as surprised as he was delighted that the 'simple' and 'gentle' Bowen therapy had caused self-correction. This is what Bowen does. It balances and stimulates the body's energy and thereby causes any necessary change. He had one more treatment and was told to come back in four weeks' time only if he had any residual twinges, because we must avoid over-treating and, thereby, undoing the beneficial work. The body will make subtle changes for some time and this varies depending upon each patient's individual constitution.

It is a pleasure to report that he telephoned to confirm all was well again and to express his gratitude.

At home, in my practice room, working on an unsuspecting patient.

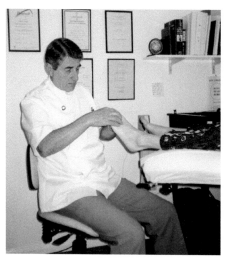

The signboard says it all; The Head Office, St Petersburg, Florida USA.

'The Boss' - President of the International Institute of Reflexology, and Nephew of The Founder, Eunice Ingham, the late Mr Dwight Byers. In his office and as cheerful as ever.

chapter four

Time Spent in Kuwait

In 1976, I was fortunate to be invited back to the EITB, not
as a senior training officer but as a fee-earning consultant
and part of a small team, with a brief to go out into industry
and work within it to demonstrate the commercial return
from efficient, monitored and evaluated training. Later, I
learned that the job was offered to me because the Board
found itself short of personnel with experience of setting
up and running a business. In a way, Prime Minister
Ted Heath had done me a favour by declaring a three-
day week and forcing my hand. His actions resulted in
paid assignments being ended overnight. This made
my company unsustainable along with a good many
subcontractors throughout commerce and manufacturing
industry in Britain at that time.

This was the background to one of my early overseas
assignments in Kuwait. I was to be one of a consortium
chosen to assist the Kuwait Oil Company set up an all-

embracing training and development centre from a 'space in the desert', helping with planning through to construction and then to commissioning.

The consortium was made up of a chartered architect, a chartered surveyor, an administrator, myself and an on-site senior manager of the oil company – an American of considerable experience of the oil industry in general and of the Kuwait Oil Company in particular. He, in turn, was supported by a Scottish gentleman of some ten years' experience of the company, who had been resident in Kuwait for a similar period of time and could speak Kuwaiti.

We were looked after very well. Throughout our stay, we had the use of a Chevrolet car, which had automatic drive, electric windows and climate control. At that time, in the late 1970s, these features were a luxury to us but essential to the Arabs in their local climate. In May to October, the typical temperature was 38° and in the July to August period it could reach 50°, with sixty to eighty per cent humidity. An air-conditioned working environment was essential.

Two temporary driving licences were issued to our team and I had one of them. Apart from adjusting to left-hand drive and driving on the right-hand side of the road, life was straightforward, figuratively speaking. However, on a trip into Kuwait City one morning, I had to play dodgems with the locals at a crossroads. Although there are uninterrupted views in the desert, the local drivers are, by nature, both impatient and volatile, so finding a safe gap to proceed needs full attention. The attention was interrupted by our Arab guide's voice from the back of the car, "If you hit another vehicle, do not stop."

"Why? What if someone is injured?" I asked.

"Never mind, do not stop, because they put you in prison while they decide who was at fault and you would not like Kuwaiti prisons and could be there a long time."

I was no longer sure that holding a licence was a privilege or such a good idea!

There was a briefing session in the early days to explain that weekends were Friday and Saturdays and that it was wise to be aware of Kuwaiti customs and etiquette. For example, the right hand is the one used for giving and receiving. It was both social and business good manners to drink two glasses of coffee before refusing a third cup. This proved very useful because the coffee was more like a strong black broth and was drunk alternately with a small glass of water. Even so, two cups of their coffee were quite enough.

An intriguing part of my time in Kuwait was the phantom nature of the house batman. I rarely caught sight of him, yet the washed and ironed laundry would be piled neatly at the end of my bed on my return in the afternoon (we started work at 7am and finished at 3pm). This ritual was followed on every day I was resident. Our accommodation in the oil company's guest quarters, together with being looked after twenty-four hours a day, was how it must have been in the days of the Empire for our diplomatic core in the countries that we administered – an almost unrealistic step back in time.

During one of our visits, one of our soccer clubs, West Bromwich Albion, were visiting pre-season and playing friendly matches in Kuwait City's magnificent national stadium. So, on my return to Britain, I approached Bristol

City (then a first-division club) and got the manager's (Alan Dicks) written permission to see if, while in Kuwait, I could arrange a game for them. There was a meeting with the Sports Minister, but, despite negotiating at that level, nothing came of it. Later, I learned it was because I had not gone through a 'middle man' or 'Wasta'. This was a valuable lesson and one to be borne in mind by any British company attempting to do business in the Gulf. Incidentally, very few British cars or vehicles were evident – BMW, Nissan, Toyota and Volkswagen were everywhere. In fact, because I was British, I was asked on more than one occasion if I could get a Land Rover! The market was there, but where were the British manufacturers? The entire time I was there, I only saw one Austin A60.

Another surprise was the gardens of the bungalows in Ahmadi, a small town to the south of Kuwait City and where we were based. The gardens in the suburbs were western in appearance, with plenty of flowers and some huge vegetables – presumably resulting from the warm sunlight.

The social life among the expats was very enjoyable and included an evening of Gilbert and Sullivan, presented by The Ahmadi Musical Society, and a visit to the Kuwaiti Little Theatre in Ahmadi to see *Don't Just Lie There, Say Something!*, written by Michael Pertwee. But enough of our privileged lifestyle; it is time to recall some of the general aspects of the state.

I found the Kuwaitis to be a proud nation, loyal and very straightforward in business matters, with an expectation of excellence in all matters. To understand this, it is useful to know a little about Kuwait's history. The word 'Kuwait' means 'a fort' and in the 1700s, the Al-Sabah family took control and built the first fortified settlement. They traded with other Arab states, internally via caravans and individual Bedouin, and with the outside world via their port and its large sailing fleet.

However, there were numerous family feuds and disputes with the Ottoman Empire and, in 1899, Britain agreed to manage foreign relations and defence for the Al-Sabah dynasty. It seems that this cooperative arrangement may have been the root of a mutual friendship between Britain and Kuwait. During our stay, there were times when they said they respected the British way of managing various situations. This surprised me and would surprise me even more in recent times, if indeed the respect for all things British still exists. Let us hope that it continues.

Kuwait's wealth could not have been created if Kuwaitis had not developed sophisticated trading expertise in the hard times of the pre-oil years. A period when harsh climate conditions and meagre resources demanded hard work and business initiatives.

The state's geographical position has provided it with excellent opportunities to trade with the outside world and its inhabitants have had long experience in commerce, from its time as a relatively small trading port to one of significance. The port was the home of a large sailing fleet that established lucrative commercial links with ports in India, East Asia and beyond. In the days of the 1950s and 1960s, it was the home of skilled craftsmen and merchants. The sheltered anchorage guaranteed its importance as a port. Trading caravans crossed the desert with merchandise from many countries and ensured its economic well-being among its neighbours who did not have the advantage of a port.

Kuwait entered the affluent age of oil well prepared as a business community, eminently capable of adjusting to a new situation that offered riches undreamed of in the age of the camel and the seagoing *dhow* (fishing smack/boat). Among the first to break their links with the traditional past and to embrace new ventures founded on the wealth from oil were the long-established merchant families. Their previous activities were associated with pearl diving, fishing, *dhow* building and regional maritime trading.

Kuwait's banking and finance grew in unison with the progressive exploration and exploitation of crude oil and its refinement. Until 1960, the currency of the state was the Indian Rupee, reflecting the history of long-established trading links between India and the Gulf States. But in 1960, the State Currency Board established the Dinar (JD) as Kuwait's currency and it remains today.

During the Iraq/Iran war, Kuwait gave considerable financial support to Iraq. Yet by 1989/90, relations between the two states had deteriorated to the point of instability, largely perhaps because of Saddam Hussein's envy of Kuwait's oil-rich wealth. Indeed, one of the quarrels that appeared to be the last straw was Iraq accusing Kuwait of 'slant-drilling' across the border into Iraq.

These threats and counter threats culminated in the invasion of Kuwait by Iraq on 2nd August 1990. They soon overran any resistance and, in so doing, commanded the oil fields, but it was short-lived. In February 1991, the coalition forces started a ground assault and Kuwait was liberated on 26th February of that year, some seven months after the initial invasion. Unfortunately, Iraq had time to cause mayhem by setting fire to many of the oil fields, but Kuwaiti people are excellent at pulling together and being focused upon what has to be done and the sustained recovery effort has been remarkable.

During the occupation, the emir and his government and many other Kuwaitis took refuge in neighbouring Saudi Arabia and in other nations. The Emir and his Ministers managed the state's affairs from Saudi, London and elsewhere, drawing on the substantial Kuwaiti investments available outside Kuwait for funding war-related expenses. The emir's return to power went relatively smoothly and he took up the reins from the end of February.

Typically, the liberation of Kuwait was the cause of great celebration and the 26th February is designated 'Liberation Day', which is celebrated annually along with National Day on 25th February. The other major celebration for Kuwaiti and other Arab Muslims is Ramadan, in which they fast for thirty days during daylight hours from sunrise to sunset. We were told, subsequently, that one of the reasons we were awarded the training centre/college contract was that our bid had taken account of Ramadan in our forecast of the time needed to complete the job to their satisfaction.

Despite a background in-house disputes and conflicts with the Ottoman Empire, Kuwait finally achieved its independence from Britain in 1961, whereupon it ended its partnership with Gulf Oil and British Petroleum (BP). A significant development, in the wake of independence, was the rapid expansion of education, which the government had controlled since

1939. The Constitution of 1962 stipulated that education would be assured and promoted by the state and that education was a fundamental rite to all citizens. Indeed, by 1960, there were approximately 45,000 students enrolled on the education system, including 18,000 girls. In 1965, schooling was made compulsory.

By 1967, private schools were re-emerging with the help of sizeable government subsidies. The system continued to expand and by 2013, it was larger than ever – boasting 500,000 students in Kuwaiti schools, nearly thirty per cent of the state's entire population.

There are three basic levels within the education system:

- Preschool – for four to six year olds.
- Elementary – four years of study for six to ten year olds.
- Intermediate – four years of study for ten to fourteen year olds.

All stages of education are free and all students study English from the age of ten years – the intermediate stage. Many of the private schools have foreign sponsors and a small sample is shown here, to show who is involved and to indicate which parts of the world regard it as a worthwhile investment:

- The Al-Bayan Bilingual School
- The American School of Kuwait
- The American International School
- The British School of Kuwait
- The French School

The system is not funded entirely by government subsidy, although it allocates land for school construction and the distribution of textbooks. In the past, it has supported education with an investment of 5.6 KD (dinars) per year.

The Kuwaiti co-ed private schools are segregated by sex, from the beginning of the first grade. A scheme launched in 1989 by the Ministry of Education saw the setting up of literacy clinics for women (they are granted the same rights as men for education).

Regarding higher education, there are two state-supported institutions:

- Kuwait University
- Public Authority for Applied Education and Training

In addition, there are a number of post-secondary colleges and universities approved by the Ministry of Education, including:

- Gulf University for Science & Technology
- Australian University
- American University of Kuwait
- Gulf American College
- Maastricht School of Management
- Box Hill College

Overall, the government ensures that each new school has a library and an expanded collection of books. For example, pre-Iraq invasion, there were 230,000 books in the schools. By 2006, this had grown to over three million books in school libraries. An 'Education Net' project has been launched with the intention of achieving a situation where every government school and library in Kuwait would be linked by a telecommunications data network. I was not aware of a similar situation in the UK at the time of our work there.

Kuwait has a comprehensive health service that is not reorganised every three years, as appears to happen in England. Equally, it does not spend an embarrassing proportion of the health budget on compensation for varying degrees of proven incompetence. Before numerous letters of protest are received, let me assure the reader that I value our NHS, not least because the incidents that make the headlines are a minority and do unfair harm to the morale of all those who do their utmost to look after us when we need it.

Kuwait's system dates from the early 1900s. It established a hospital for men in 1911 and for women in 1919, and between then until 1946 there was a dramatic improvement in health conditions with a corresponding improvement in life expectancy – in 1990, it was seventy-two years for males and seventy-six years for females. When you consider the heat and dust of the environment, this seems very commendable. Mortality rates fell in unison with the increased life expectancy. By the 1950s, Kuwait had a free healthcare system in place, which included veterinary medicine. It relied heavily upon foreign workers, just as our system has a similar reliance today.

The state expenditure on health ranked 3rd in the national budget, behind public works and education. By 1990, the level of investment enabled it to provide free medical service from highly trained practitioners working in modern facilities.

Perhaps when we think or speak of the Arab States, we think of oil, and it is oil that is the major source of income for Kuwait. By 1952, Kuwait had become the largest exporter of crude oil in the Persian Gulf – drawing in workers from overseas, particularly from Egypt and India. It nationalised its oil industry in the 1970s and ended the partnership it had with Gulf Oil and with British Petroleum (BP), and became a member of the Organisation of Petroleum Exporting Countries (OPEC). This is the organisation that sets the price of crude oil per barrel, based upon the prevailing supply and demand worldwide. The price the consumer pays, seems to me, to be influenced by a kind of financial stock market, whereby a degree of manipulation exists between those with the greatest influence within the fuel distribution market, who use that influence to achieve the greatest returns for the nebulous 'middle men' in the chain of events from producer to consumer.

By 2010, Kuwait was the fourth-largest exporter (by volume) of oil in OPEC and remained heavily dependent upon it. The revenue from petroleum revenues accounting for half of its gross domestic product (GDP), ninety-five per cent of total earnings and ninety-five per cent of government revenues.

At the beginning of 2011, Kuwait had an estimated 101.5 billion barrels of proven oil reserves and held five billion barrels of reserves in the 'neutral zone' with neighbouring Saudi Arabia on a fifty/fifty basis (ref: *Oil & Gas Journal* of January 2011, Kuwait).

In addition, the state has a Sovereign Wealth Fund that

means it allocates ten per cent of state revenues into the 'Reserve Fund for Future Generations' (RFFG) for the time when oil income starts to decline. It would be reassuring to know whether Britain made similar provision for the time when the income from North Sea oil and gas declines. This far-sighted approach is reflected in a persistent drive to become self-sufficient, not least in the sufficient supply of water for drinking or for irrigation, and this is done in a coordinated way. For example, water and electricity generation flow in partnership.

Oil-powered stations generate electricity and water, a dual-purpose facility. Boilers generate steam at high pressure and temperature, and this is used to drive steam turbine generators to produce electricity. After doing most of its work, the steam is taken as low energy heating for the distillation plants to produce distilled water.

Back in the late 1970s, when I was there, many western cities and countries were extremely interested in this integrated system of energy generation and the production of distilled water in large quantities. At that time, New York, San Francisco, Britain and Hong Kong were among those seeking advice on Kuwait's desalination plants. It is unclear what happened to Britain's interest in the interim period. Despite being an island, desalination plants remain sparse, while floods cost us thousands and the unfortunate people affected are caused a great deal of misery and inconvenience. Short-term government, by whatever political party, is the antithesis of long-term planning and investment necessary for efficient national provision of energy infrastructure and flood prevention.

Regarding the push towards self-sufficiency, Kuwait's

long-term aim is to produce sufficient food to feed its population, or at least to get as close as possible to that ideal situation. It consumes approximately 25,000 tons of tomatoes and 10,000 tons of cucumbers every year – so it is not surprising that to burp is considered a sign of a meal enjoyed!

In the 1970s, home production accounted for about thirteen per cent of the total domestic consumption, leaving a large gap to be filled by imports. Despite deficiencies of soil, the relative shortage of irrigation water and challenging climatic conditions, the state's ambitious target could be achieved due to the people's focus, determination, overall wealth and cumulative effort.

The ambition to produce as much home-grown produce as conditions would allow was sparked by the establishment of the Kuwait Experimental Farm in 1953. In its early days, it occupied 1,000 square metres and that land became the gardens in the centre of the farm, as it expanded to cover approximately seventy-five hectares. Its earlier work focused upon finding out which types of plant, shrubs and trees could survive or thrive. As water became more plentiful, the activities of the farm expanded. First, by increasing the area under cultivation and then into breeding poultry, cattle and other livestock.

By the late 1970s, the farm operated under the aegis of the Department of Agriculture and included plant production, horticulture, hydroponics, irrigation, forestry, pastures, animal husbandry and beekeeping. In addition, the farm had supervision of the state's zoological gardens. The future continues to be exciting and promises an excellent return on the collaborative investment of time, money, research and effort.

Overseeing Kuwait's significant and various activities is its government, which, in turn, is subservient to the emir. Unfortunately, the emir reigning during the time we were there was ill with a form of cancer and this necessitated him being flown to Britain on numerous occasions to receive treatment from one of our London hospitals. In October of 1977, the emir returned from London and there was huge celebration and excitement. I remember we were driven into Kuwait City by our Kuwaiti guide. When we headed back to Ahmadi, our driver told us to look out for the wild and unpredictable driving of other vehicles. Sure enough, he had no sooner alerted us than a whole cluster of vehicles sped past us by driving off-road on the sand beside the road surface, creating clouds of sand like a mini sandstorm and accompanied by many horns sounding and people shouting.

Sadly, after our return to Britain, between work on-site, the emir died in December of that year. What we had not realised was that upon the death of an emir, all contracts are terminated and so ended our contract for the construction of their comprehensive education and training centre based in Ahmadi, south of Kuwait city.

The State of Kuwait has been ruled by the Al-Sabah dynasty since around 1752. The constitution, approved in 1962, called for direct elections to the National Assembly and relatively free and fair elections to the assembly are held on a regular basis.

Kuwait is not a democracy by the usual definition of the word because the Prime Minister is not responsible to parliament but to the emir, as we will see below. However, Kuwaitis enjoy more civil and political freedoms than citizens of most non-democratic states. Its parliament is the strongest of those found in the monarchies of the Gulf. They take great pride in the rarity of political violence in their country, especially given the high levels of violence found frequently in neighbouring states and elsewhere in the Arab world.

The power of the emir is considerable and was defined, as distinct from being handed down, by the 1961 Constitution. It includes:

- appointing the Prime Minister.
- dissolving parliament.
- promulgating laws.
- referring bills back to parliament for reconsideration.
- appointing military officers.

Succession to the throne is limited to the descendants of the great Mubarak Al-Sabah. The reigning emir must appoint an heir apparent within one year of his accession to the throne and the nomination must be approved by a majority of members of the National Assembly. The heir apparent has to be at least thirty years of age on the date of his royal proclamation, of sound mind and the legitimate son of Muslim parents.

Traditionally, the position of emir is alternated between the two main branches of the Al-Sabah family; the Al-Jaber and the Al-Salem branches. The emir, since January 2006, is His Highness Sabah Al-Ahmad Al-Jaber Al-Sabah.

In the twelve years to 1977, Kuwait experienced an

unprecedented era of prosperity under the rule of Sabah Al-Salin Al-Sabah, who died in December 1977, and under his successor, who died in January 2006. During their reign, the country was transformed into a highly developed welfare state with a free market economy.

In addition to its comprehensive healthcare system, the government provides one of the world's most encompassing social service systems. Not only does it support the nation indirectly through guaranteed state employment and subsidised services – water and electricity – but it supports those most in need through direct subsidies. These include the disabled, the elderly, the unemployed, students and their families, the widowed, the unmarried and the families of prisoners.

I have never felt as safe during the day or night as when I was living in Kuwait. This was because I was fortunate to experience a country that has laws it does not hesitate to implement. If you digress, you pay the penalty. In some instances, it can be swift and severe, but you know where you stand.

The irony is that to be free requires boundaries of behaviour set clearly by strict law. The price of freedom hinges on accepting both personal and corporate responsibility for our actions within those boundaries, which, in turn, set the standards of social behaviour generally.

Laissez-faire seems attractive but is a mirage that can lead, ultimately, to a society in which no one cares anymore.

Kuwait City's soccer stadium, 1976

Buildimg for the future: the window lintels of the buildings on the left appear to be upside down

A scene on the outskirts of Kuwait City. The picturesque facade contrasts what may lay behind the main building, 1976

Graceful water towers, 1976

These two pictures are of gardens in Ahmadi, south of Kuwait City, but still in the desert. They could be in England; just shows what can be achieved with regular watering! 1976

chapter five

The Bosnian Experience

Before mentioning my brief, but salutary, experience of the part of the Balkans known as Bosnia and Herzegovina, it helps to recall some of the recent history of this area of fragile peace.

When World War II swept into the Balkans, Hungary, Romania, Bulgaria and Albania were allied with the axis countries of Germany and Italy. Initially, Yugoslavia joined them, but when anti-Nazi Serbians took over the government in 1941, the German Army invaded. The Yugoslav resistance, including the Communist Party, worked against the German occupants for the remainder of the war. This resistance was led by Josip Broz Tito, who held the country together before the tragic splintering that took place later.

After the war, the Soviets broke with Tito. They had imposed Soviet-style communism and created the Iron Curtain to strengthen its grip. Tito chose to apply a maverick communism and his own ideas for Pan-Slavic cooperation in Yugoslavia. Unfortunately, Tito – the 'glue' that held Yugoslavia together – died in 1980 and by 1990 communism had collapsed.

Serbia was pressing for control once again and with no overall vision to keep it together, Yugoslavia splintered in a series of violent and ethnically charged conflicts that led to a bloody civil war in 1992, which lasted for four years in varying degrees of ferocity and at a number of locations. United Nations (UN) forces tried to sort out the conflict but found it surprisingly difficult.

Ethnic squabbles have been going on for years in the Balkans. World War I was started when a Serbian nationalist assassinated Archduke Franz Ferdinand, the Austro-Hungarian heir. A month later, Austria-Hungary declared war on Serbia, and it spread from there as other countries took sides and were drawn into the conflict.

The Bosnian War was said to have started from an innocent young girl being shot as she crossed a bridge over the river that runs through Sarajevo; the shot coming from the Serbs in the mountains that surround the city. They had gathered there in ever-increasing numbers under the guise of army manoeuvres. Ultimately, UN forces became involved.

The make-up of the population of Bosnia and Herzegovina compounded the difficulties faced by the UN troops. Bosnia's Muslims or Bosnians trace their ancestry to Christian Slavic people, who converted to Islam during the Otterman Empire. Serbs and Croats have each claimed the land as their own. Hence their rivalry is deep-seated. To end that rivalry, socialist Yugoslavia recognised Bosnians as a separate people in 1969. Before the latest war, they made up an estimated thirty-eight per cent of Bosnia and Herzegovina's population; Serbs made up forty per cent and Croats, twenty-two per cent.

Conflict simmered up to and beyond World War II. Competing ethnic claims, based on history, led to civil war after Bosnia and Herzegovina split from Yugoslavia in 1992. Serbia and Croatia each sent in troops, but the Serbs saw their chance to exercise their long-held desire to dominate by cleansing the country of Croats and Bosnians. The UN resolved to restore peace and some form of democracy by intervening militarily. But the complex make-up of the population was not as clear-cut as described earlier.

There were Serbs and Croats and Serbo-Croatian speaking southern Slavs. The Croats, however, are mostly Roman Catholic and use the Latin alphabet of Western Europe. On the other hand, Serbs tend to be Orthodox Christians who use the Cyrillic alphabet of Eastern Europe. These differences have divided the two communities for years.

During World War II, Axis-aligned Croatia persecuted and killed Serbs among other ethnic groups and the Serb-dominated resistance retaliated.

Against this background of bitter differences, it is a little easier to understand the civil war of the 1990s and the whole confusion in which UN forces were charged with restoring order, together with as much understanding and peace as was possible. But the land was quite literally a minefield. We need to understand that the conflict took place among a population that was a mix of Serbs (whose aim was to regain dominance and to eliminate any opposition), Croats and Bosnians, all with scores to settle. Add the Roman Catholics among the Croats, Orthodox Christians among the Serbs and some Muslims, and it was difficult to know who was who and whose cause the UN were supposed to be supporting. Chaos!

My time in Bosnia arose from charity work initially. A local doctor in Sarajevo requested that someone train his team of physiotherapists in one of the therapies being used. The well-meaning volunteers and the sheer diverse range of expertise offered was causing some confusion to him and his staff. For whatever reason, reflexology got the nod and the request to train and work in unison with his medical centre staff came to the International Institute of Reflexology (IIR) in the UK. At that time I was UK Vice President, while Mr Dwight Byers was based at the United States Headquarters in St Petersburg, Florida. The UK-based charity was to provide the financial support to enable us to do the work, which was beyond our normal scope of activity.

Our first glimpse of Bosnia, and Sarajevo in particular, was in early February 1998, as the aircraft from Vienna descended between the mountains that surround the city. It was natural curiosity to stare from the aeroplane window to get a first glimpse of a war-torn countryside. Buildings with severely damaged roofs and many without roofs, while others had been reduced to a heap of rubble. All represented the collective scars of recent conflict, while hiding the human loss and suffering.

Snow-covered Sarajevo Airport greeted us with basic facilities and an outside temperature of -9° as my colleague, Linda Rumbles, and I checked through customs. We were in Sarajevo as representatives of the IIR. The purpose was to provide basic practitioner training and qualifications – by the IIR's examination standard – to a team of qualified and practising physiotherapists. This would enable them to be self-sufficient in treating the widespread trauma cases caused by and during the Bosnian War.

The war had ended two years prior in 1996 and the city was recovering itself with the aid of a number of European countries and of Japan, which, linked to the European initiatives, supplied a fleet of modern buses. British involvement was visible in the continued restoration of mains supplies of gas, electricity, water and other allied services, as well as the removal of landmines and the reopening of roads in the surrounding area.

During our first visit, I was walking in the city with another British charity volunteer, when he sensed my curiosity regarding a nearby church that somehow had survived apparently unscathed. He immediately offered a restraining arm and a warning to stay well clear because the churchyard would be another likely minefield and no one could be sure which areas had been cleared and declared safe. Similarly, we were not allowed to venture into the surrounding countryside.

The trains and trolley buses were running again and were amazingly frequent – carrying passengers in or out of the city. It is ironic, but not surprising, that the service would have been the envy of many of Britain's cities. For example, during our time in Bosnia, Bristol was still debating whether and where to have a form of tram service. Maybe some of our councils could learn a thing or two from Sarajevo's public transport system. The vehicles were ancient – except those supplied by Japan (where was the UK?) – and basic, with non-upholstered metal seats. Although, despite the recent shortages, some residents carried their own in-built upholstery and were broad across the beam. But the system served their public to its apparent satisfaction and we were grateful for it.

Arrangements had been made for us to stay at the home of one of the physiotherapists, who would act as our interpreter during much of our stay and certainly during the training modules.

She was a kind and charming young lady, Fikreta Lelovic (nicknamed Vicki), to whom we owe a great deal of thanks. Without Fikreta's help, the whole programme would not have been possible. Equally kind and generous with her time and help was Vicki's mother, Yasma. Vicki's brother and younger sister were also helpful and lived at home. The house bore the scars of war in the form of bullet marks in the plaster of the outside walls and one major mark where a rocket fired from a helicopter had smashed through the front wall – first beneath the window – travelled across the lounge/living area and smashed into the kitchen beyond.

Yasma still trembled with fear at the sound of any helicopter in their vicinity; hardly surprising because the rocket had narrowly missed her youngest daughter as she slept. There were many more similar stories, which we became privy to as the local people became familiar with what we were doing and we gained their trust.

Regarding the training programme, all the hand-out material for the six modules was translated from the USA/ UK version into Bosnian prior to each respective visit. For this, we were indebted to Lada Copic for the invaluable help she provided throughout the entire programme.

The physiotherapists started every day, Monday to Friday, at 8am and their day finished at 3pm, with voluntary extra sessions done on some Saturdays to cope with demand. After a rest of half an hour, their reflexology training was undertaken on three consecutive evenings; these finished between 6.30pm and 7pm, depending upon the degree of tiredness of the students. There was no point in working beyond the stage of glazed facial expressions.

At the beginning, teaching was done in a somewhat confined space of the old medical centre and, on the subsequent visits, it was conducted in the new medical centre which was about half a mile from the old one.

Unfortunately, between our first and second visits there was a misunderstanding between the funding charity and ourselves. It had promised to back the whole project financially. But before our second trip out to Bosnia, some of their staff had reported that the physiotherapists had not done the interim study and practice to take them to the next stage and they pulled out and stopped the funding. This had two effects; one, that the person who was adamant that the money was there to complete the programme did not have the authority to pledge the support; two, unless we undertook to finance and complete their training, the physiotherapists would be left high and dry and our reputation would be damaged. Consequently, we decided to complete the job and to assess the situation ourselves.

On our next and second visit, it was clear why no further study or practice had been done. Simply, they were all too busy, coping with their heavy patient-loads, many of whom had lingering trauma problems from the war years in addition to the need for continuing physical treatment. However, we found that with their untiring interest and determination, they caught up by the end of the first week of training.

The underlying problem, I believe, was that our UK charity personnel had applied a British standard of expectancy while failing to appreciate or grasp the reality that we faced because of the prevailing situation on the ground in Sarajevo. The situation demanded that we had to adapt while not lowering standards of proficiency or professionalism and attitudes among the physiotherapists. While we worked alongside them during the day and taught them in the evenings, their energy and enthusiasm was first class and made up for any temporary lapse between our first and second visit. The IIR (UK) was now funding the programme, under the approval of the local medical officer of Health Sarajevo and director of the medical centre, Dr Muftic.

Lecture sessions were conducted on-site with a physiotherapist who acted as a translator throughout – Fikreta Lelovic. She managed to combine her own learning with translating for her friends and colleagues. We had to trust that any emphasis we made was not lost in translation. Their facial expressions and body language suggested that Fikreta did a marvellous job.

We were surprised to find a relatively low level of understanding of anatomy and physiology compared to their UK counterparts. It had been assumed that we could summarise this aspect and so provide greater time to perfect the techniques of reflexology, as practised by certified members of the IIR. Again, this deficiency needed to be understood and it had a two-pronged background. One, their earlier training and studies had been severely disturbed by the conflict. It is difficult – if not impossible to study – when under threat from mortar fire, tanks and small-arms fire! Secondly, they were shy and reluctant to admit what they did not know. We were pleased to help, both to gain their confidence and to spend extra time to assist them to overcome any deficit and to make good the 'gap' over which they had had no control.

The rewarding aspect throughout was their enthusiasm and dedication. I wish we could have bottled it and prescribed it to those of our youth who lack the confidence and sense of achievement that stems from being given a tangible opportunity.

We all react, to some extent, to climatic conditions. On the first trip in February, the air temperature was a high of −9° and it snowed most days; on the second visit – in June – the temperature was 32°, plus high humidity. In those latter conditions, to apply any form of physical therapy for six or seven hours a day is very tiring, yet we were asking our physiotherapists to do that and then to study with us for a further three hours. Their endurance and perseverance enabled them to cope with the demands placed upon them to the extent that they completed modules three and four and managed a verbal mock theory examination. This was with the best of intensions on our part, but it did threaten to resurrect the fear of having to admit to gaps in their knowledge.

The visit in October introduced us to weather that

varied from mixed to winter cold. In the final weeks, the physiotherapists took the written and practical examinations. These examinations were to the institute's normal standard of diplomas, with a theory pass mark of eighty per cent. This may be a surprise to some readers, but it is to ensure that students are thoroughly competent and of a standard to look after patients' welfare and to stand alongside those in established medicine. The only difference with the Bosnian theory paper was that it was based on the handouts we had given the students, because there were, at that time, no reflexology textbooks in their native language.

The draft examination paper in English, with its marking schedule, was submitted to the head office in Florida, USA, for approval and, as such, followed established and usual procedure. Upon return, it was sent for translation into Bosnian so that both the examination paper and its marking schedule were in Bosnian. Arrangements had been made by the medical director of the medical centres in Sarajevo for an appointed independent medic to do the marking – thus removing any suspicion of favouritism. There was a mutual all-round wish that all the students would be successful. The amount of work they put in between and during our visits to Bosnia had been phenomenal and we were very proud of each of them.

At each period spent in Sarajevo during 1998, we worked alongside the physiotherapists and treated members of the public, who received treatment free at the point of delivery. During my last trip, I had a 'block' of fifteen patients within two days. Thirty to forty treatments per week was the usual work schedule; many of the patients were treated daily by the physiotherapists and afterwards came for reflexology.

There were some tragic cases. Almost everyone had a tragic or traumatic experience from the war years. Some would relay them – often tearfully; some would keep their story to themselves. Eighteen months after the end of the war, many of the patients we saw were still suffering trauma. Maybe they would suffer for the rest of their lives and certainly they would never forget. The scars of war can be varied and often tragic.

Yet there were also some very humble and satisfying experiences. The lady whose shoulder pain was eased for the first time in over a year and who, as a consequence, had enjoyed her first uninterrupted full night's sleep since the war. Via our interpreter, her effused thanks were embarrassing and satisfying in equal measure. Another lady, who suffered from arthritis, benefitted after just the initial session and returned the following morning with a broad smile and a spontaneous hug. I thought that if they all reacted so spontaneously, I was in for a very pleasant time! What transpired was that this lady had less pain, more movement and warmth in her body for the first time in her life. There were numerous similar improvements in increased mobility, decreased pain and general all-round well-being and her general demeanour was calmer compared to when she first attended.

The response from many of the patients was humbling and the extent of the thanks was a wonderful surprise. One lady said, through our English-speaking physiotherapist, "God bless you. You have made my feet and legs warm and mobile and with less pain for the first time in twenty years.

How can I possibly thank you?" I took her hands in mine, looked her in the eyes and said, "That is thanks enough." She became one of the regulars.

One patient fell asleep for twenty minutes of their treatment – I had not realised I was that boring! Clearly, she was mentally and physically exhausted and needed to switch off. Another was almost in tears when she came for the second treatment and described that she had had the first pain-free night in a long, long time. Her left shoulder was so much less painful that she could not thank me enough, so she would be bringing tomorrow's breakfast to the medical centre for me and the other physiotherapists.

Patients bringing gifts for medical staff at the centre was a common practice. Usually it was chocolates, cigarettes, cakes of all sizes and flavours, and sometimes special hand-made dishes for a complete lunch or a brunch. Physiotherapists enjoyed this flow of food during every chance they had for a break and at lunchtime they added cigarette smoke to the menu. You could not see clearly across the room.

A reflexology treatment can cause the patient's individual constitution to seek balance, homeostasis, and in doing so can produce an adverse reaction initially. In the UK, I have known this to disturb the person sufficiently to end further sessions, despite a warning that this may occur, and an explanation of why it can occur and the longer-term benefit. It is the body getting rid of rubbish – a process of self-corrective cleansing. It was Hippocrates who was credited as saying, "Give me a fever and I can cure the illness". In other words, a phenomena with which we are familiar; that there is often a time during an illness when we feel worse and this can be just prior to the beginning of feeling much healthier.

This was the background that one of the Bosnian patients experienced. He was asthmatic and came to me on a Friday for his first reflexology treatment. Again, I called the interpreter to us to explain the possibility of an initial adverse reaction. He returned the following Monday and said he had spent the weekend being sick and coughing up phlegm, but then laughed and said, "But today I feel better than for years. I want more of what you do Englishman."

Two things are worth mentioning at this time. One, these results could not be cast aside as placebo effect – a term used in a somewhat dismissive tone by some in the established mainstream of medicine in the UK. Two, because of the language barrier, I could not have otherwise influenced the outcome by some kind of hypnotic effect. Although, this is not to deny that, as in any form of health treatment, the restoration of morale, hope and a good slice of positive optimism can be a wonderful aid to recovery.

It was indeed refreshing to work in an environment that was not preoccupied with the need for scientific evidence and research. Everyone – particularly the medical director – was concerned only with the care of the patient, by whatever professional technique. The patients' concern was to be treated and we regarded each of them as a person of equal standing, who deserved our sympathy and understanding. In such an environment, the public and the doctor accept any improvement that can be seen with their own eyes, backed by what the patients tell them. In short, everyone was too busy getting on with the job – there was little or no time to stand, stare or criticise. The full-time medical staff, as far as I experienced, were no less dedicated than our NHS staff. The big difference was that they were not overburdened nor hindered by layers of administration, remote 'managers' and the social 'disease' of bureaucracy.

Equally, patients could be embarrassingly grateful and would emphasise their gratitude with unsolicited and unexpected gifts of chocolates, fruit, or even free breakfasts or lunches! Apparently, this was normal practice for the physiotherapists at the medical centre.

Although I was in Sarajevo for a relatively short time, from February to October 1998, the city and its suburbs showed tangible signs of recovery via mine clearance and the repair of buildings and starts on new ones. Yet there remained areas of great contrast; it was possible to stand in a main street and look at a devastated apartment block; turn your back on them and you could see old buildings that, somehow, had remained unscathed; or you might be looking at a brand new building rising up as a defiant symbol of the power of human recovery.

Much of the old part of the city remained intact despite the heavy bombardment that left its bullet pock marks on the facade of those buildings, as if they had suffered chickenpox.

While peace existed officially, it was reinforced by the visible presence of the UN's troops. They were even more evident towards the end of 1998 because Kosovo had become unstable due to dominant behaviour of Slobodan Milošević. Everyone was mentally prepared for anything and it was impressed upon us to carry our passports at all times, night or day. There was a strange atmosphere created by a mixture of extreme friendliness and a genuine welcome towards us, yet at the same time, an underlying tension among the local population. Perhaps this had its roots set too deeply in ethnic and religious differences for it to be otherwise.

My last visit in October 1998 proved an interesting experience. Dr Muftic had assured me that he would arrange accommodation away from the physiotherapists to ensure there would be no possibility of favouritism when it came to examination time. I was curious to see what had transpired. The flight details had been forwarded and the plane was on time. The journey was smooth, except for a choppy descent into Sarajevo, which was quite usual because of the mountainous area around the city.

A dull, grey sky and heavy rain greeted me on my 3pm arrival, but no one else did. Initially, I took a wrong turn after passport clearance into the security checkout and had to re-route to the exit. I was nearly despatched before I'd arrived.

Again, no known person in sight, so I approached what turned out to be a friendly policeman who kindly hailed a taxi. I waived one of Dr Muftic's business cards at the driver, smiled and said, "Clinic, *molin*" ("Clinic, please"). We were off, hopefully in the correct direction and by the shortest route.

Having got to the clinic, there was more gloom – to match the incessant rain. It was totally deserted, not a doctor or physiotherapist anywhere. It closed at 3pm! But there was the cleaning lady with her vacuum cleaner going full blast and making a noise somewhat similar to a jet at take-off. Instant trauma was caused to the lady who, much to my amazement, recognised me. Probably because I was the cause of her having to work late on previous visits as all teaching was done after hours. She also remembered 'reflexology' and pronounced the word clearly and correctly with a wide smile of instant communication.

The cleaning lady was able to telephone Dr Muftic at his home, but he was not there. A mystery voice told me over the phone, as it was passed to me, "Stay there and my friend will come and also provide a room for the night." If they had got their wires crossed, this could be interesting!

The friend turned out to be Yasma Lelovic (our translator's mother and our kind landlady on previous visits). I was never more pleased to see a friend and we dragged my heavy suitcase for approximately half a mile uphill all the way to Yasma's apartment.

Having begun to dry out, there was a telephone call to say that my apartment was ready for me and that Vicki (Fikreta) would get a taxi and take me there that evening. We arrived at the place, which was on the side of a mountain – or so it seemed. It was now very dark with few working street lights, and it was still raining like a monsoon. In addition to the steep, narrow, unlit road, we had to negotiate a multitude of concrete steps that resembled a mini waterfall, which took us up and along the outside of a three-storey house to a side veranda and a front door.

The owners were a lovely elderly couple, but they didn't speak a single word of English. My dozen or so Bosnian words did not seem to convey any meaning either – strange, they had worked before. Perhaps my hosts were deaf? Life was about to become an unpredictable episode.

The 'apartment' comprised a lounge/bedroom, a kitchen with nowhere to cook, no cutlery and no china, a refrigerator that did not work and a TV set in the same condition. The settee in the lounge pulled out to make a double bed. My dear hosts returned at 11pm (which was late for them) and made up the bed. Where had I been until that hour? At a good friend's flat; I had her address, the taxi had waited, so off we went to the address written on a scrap of paper, dropping Vicki off en route. My friend was a reiki therapist and part of the volunteer team working at the clinic. After the meal, she said the safest mode of transport at night for the return journey to my new 'apartment' was a taxi, which she summoned by telephone having lived in the area for some time. Another scrap of paper for the taxi driver and off we went. He got lost and had to ask for directions twice from fellow taxi drivers. It was at this point that the worrying thought occurred of how easy it is to kidnap a foreign national!

Faced with no choice, you can only trust and enjoy the farce of the journey. The taxi driver asked for help from his colleagues by stopping alongside them in the middle of the road, where upon on each occasion they had quite a long chat – presumably taking the opportunity to exchange local gossip. However, to his credit, we got back to the apartment somehow. Up the numerous concrete steps and into the cold apartment, then into bed. By this time I was too tired to care much about anything and was soon sleeping soundly.

What had happened was that Dr Muftic had forgotten to meet me at the airport and a Swedish international Red Cross worker was in the top flat where I was meant to be. He would move out in two nights' time apparently; meanwhile, I remained in my basic temporary accommodation, but without food!

The following morning, I located some shops nearby and set out to buy some bits and pieces. Buying a jar of honey proved to be a challenge as the shopkeeper spoke no English and my Bosnian was basic, fragmented and clearly of no use in the shop. So, I flapped my arms and made a buzzing noise that I hoped was close enough for a bee to do the trick. No chance; judging by his facial expression, he classed me as a complete idiot from some foreign land. But, never despair, he produced a jar of honey, so facial expressions can be deceptive.

Encouraged by our new method of communication, I decided to get some eggs. Alas, there were none in sight that I could pick up or point to. So, it was back to miming; this time, flapping arms up and down in unison with chicken cackling noises that I could always do sufficiently accurately to amuse the grandchildren. He was not amused, but by this time we had been joined in the shop by one of the locals, who cottoned onto this weird, flapping, squawking stranger and got the shopkeeper to produce a small box of eggs. At that point, I decided to bail out and be thankful for what I had.

Elsewhere, bread rolls were purchased, so that on return to the flat all I needed was a knife with which to cut them down to an edible size. Miming to the landlady went more smoothly this time and she offered a lethal-looking sheath knife and a small cutting board.

Mentally, I had christened my hosts Mr and Mrs Bosnian. On my return upstairs to my room, they positively invaded my place – bringing a napkin, knife, fork, dessert spoon and a teaspoon. Luxury beckoned as, in no time, they rearranged the kitchen area, produced a low table from another room and placed plates, dishes and a cup and saucer upon it. I now had a 'kitchen diner'.

A few days later, on my return from a busy day at the new medical centre, I moved into the flat on the top floor of the house. This was relatively high up because the house was built on a steep hill and this was definitely up the slope. In addition to being on the top floor, it was approached by a steep path and, finally, by a flight of outside concrete steps that had no guide rail – quite tricky after dark until I got the hang of it. Entry was by a glass-panelled door, but more on that later!

The accommodation consisted of three rooms in line, front to back. The front door opened into a lounge area, with a couple of wicker chairs. At the back was a bedroom with a king-sized double bed, built-in wardrobe and cupboards. These rooms were separated by a kitchen diner from which the adjacent bathroom and toilet lead off. There was an outside balcony from which there was a panoramic view across the suburbia of Sarajevo.

That was the good news. The bad news was there was no drainer or sink unit in the kitchen area, neither was there water piped to the kitchen. There was one water tap for hot or cold supply, which was over a very small knees-under-chin-sized bath with shower, or rather a flexible hose with a spray-head. All washing of dishes and cutlery had to be done in the red plastic bowl placed upon a low wooden cabinet adjacent to the four-ring electric cooker.

During my first evening meal in my new residence,

a grey smudge appeared on an onion as it was cut. The grey smudge was dirt or thick dust. The top of the cooker, on closer inspection, could not be used until cleaned thoroughly. This led to a close examination of the bath, shower and toilet seat. All were surfaced with what can only be described as body grime. The next few hours were spent cleaning the flat as thoroughly as possible, in a mood of depression exaggerated by hunger. A personal 'kit' of clean plates, a fruit bowl, glass tumbler, mug, cup and saucer, knife, fork, dessert spoon and teaspoon was assembled for immediate and future use. The rest could remain untouched by human hand. The previous occupant must have been the most unhygienic Red Cross worker on the planet.

Some sort of routine was established and soon the weekend was upon us; time to relax or, more precisely, time to tackle the laundry. There was no washing powder, so back to the shops. I was met by the poor shopkeeper's expression of 'Oh, not him again'. This time, I had the forethought to take a clean handkerchief to communicate. By rubbing it, I conveyed the need to wash and, therefore, needed washing powder (again, none was visible on the shelves). However, this time it was plain sailing. The washing powder was produced. Next, some pegs; demonstrated by putting first and second fingers over the edge of my life-saving handkerchief in an inverted 'V'. He got the message. This miming business was a piece of cake – who needs to learn the language?

After the clothes were washed, they were ready to hang on the line. Fortunately, I ran a damp cloth along it first and removed more dusty grime. The line was along the length of the balcony. You would have thought that a plastic clothes peg was the same the world over. Not these, the first three snapped and my underpants nearly floated down three floors.

After these minor adventures, a daily and a weekly pattern were established and a somewhat complacent attitude prevailed, until the glass-panelled door took revenge. I had spent a pleasant evening in Sarajevo with a fellow therapist, the lady reiki healer. Unfortunately, her 'distant healing' did not reach the glazed front door of the flat. We went our separate ways after the meal and I travelled back to the flat via one of the frequent tramcars that run late into the night, every night. I got back well after dark, at about 10.30pm. I went along the street with no street lights, up the hill to the house, up the path alongside the building, up the pitch-black concrete steps, unlocked the front door, went in, closed the door, but the door jammed and would not close shut. I pushed it, then pushed it harder. No good, so I slammed it shut, whereupon all the glass shattered – and when a door does that, the glass falls down vertically, rather than scatters. I cursed and waited to see if anyone had been disturbed. Not a sound – good. I went to bed; it could be sorted in the morning.

The damage was reported to my host the following morning by indicating to him to follow me to the disaster area. I explained as best I could how it had happened and that, of course, it would be paid for. Much smiling and shrugging of shoulders and, thankfully, no blows. He did not seem too concerned. The glass had sounded loose from the outset and, maybe, he had found the idiot he hoped for who would fund the inevitable replacement. Mr Bosnian pulled out a few shards of glass and, having refused my offer of gloves, he cut his finger. Shame-faced, I had no plasters, so offered some salve.

Later that Sunday morning, Mr and Mrs Bosnian invited me down for coffee – the type that is strong enough to stand alone. Out came the family photographs and chocolate (what a splendid custom) and some delicious home-grown, home-prepared cherry fruit juice. Mr B then unwrapped his bandaged forefinger to reveal cigarette tobacco bound over the wound. Apparently, this acts as an absorbent and so another lesson was learned. Later, I checked with the locals at the medical centre and it is common practice here. Subsequently, I found out that it was common practice in World War I and was used as first aid prior to receiving medical treatment.

When both Mr and Mrs Bosnia were present at the shattered glass scene, it gave me the chance of waiving an iron over the dining room table – the only suitable flat surface available – to signal that there was no ironing board. This set Mrs B into 'instruction mode', sending her husband into the bedroom where, from the top of the wardrobe, he produced an ironing board that he very kindly assembled, ready for use. Another piece of routine had fallen into place.

During one of our ritual Sunday morning coffee breaks in their part of the house, Mr Bosnia showed me a vicious-looking piece of jagged shrapnel that had hit their house during the war – fired by the Serbs from the hill on the opposite side of the valley. The price of an uninterrupted view. He explained how he, his wife and son sheltered in a corner of the house on the middle floor during bombing or heavy shelling. They crouched in a corner, almost under the added shelter of the hillside, until they were confident that the danger had passed. Clearly, they had no time for the Serbs, yet thankfully they showed me genuine warmth and hospitality. Such experience brings a mixture of humility and gratefulness.

Then, out of the blue and out of a drawer, Mrs Bosnia produced a glass jar and with great pride showed me six of the largest gall stones I have ever seen. Each was the size of a sugar lump with well-rounded corners. Then she pulled out her clothes and pulled them up to show me the vertical scar at her midriff and smiled to convey pleasure at the neat work of the surgeon. We had met only a few days previously. Clearly, I had gained her trust and confidence and I started to wonder what else I might be shown.

At the medical centre, patients were queuing for treatment – on the previous trip it took three days before they started to queue. Now they asked for 'the Englishman' and there was a very flattering following. All days were busy with a bank of regulars. Back at the flat, the repair to the door would be the equivalent of £24, which represented four meals out or an extra four home-cooked meals to balance the books. The door would be taken off and sent away to a place down the hill where the glass would be fitted. These details were translated to me by a new lodger, a trainee lawyer, who spoke good English and was a great help. He added a comment made by Mr Bosnia that the door would be replaced as soon as possible to prevent women visitors. I joked, "In that case, leave the door off."

A memorable patient was a huge woman of approximately 6 ft tall with wrists the size of a man's ankle and ankles the size of most people's knee joint. The attached feet were my territory. If she had been a ship, it would have been an oil-tanker of 500,000 ton draft. At the foot-end, doing my best reflexology, the view was one of two large hills, beyond which was a head adorned with bushy eyebrows. Consciousness was conveyed by occasional grunts; the louder the grunt, the more severe the pain, or the word 'puno' (pain) or 'puno bolli' (much pain). It was in this primitive but effective way that any constitutional imbalance was indicated and could be treated appropriately.

A gentleman patient – a jolly man – with two fingers missing from one hand complained, via our interpreter, of stomach upsets. I worked the whole system thoroughly and warned him that he may feel worse before he felt better. Three days later, he returned and said he'd been sick and had diarrhoea since treatment. To which I replied, "Good." This shocked him until I reminded him of my warning and went on to explain that now his body had got rid of the rubbish, things would improve (which they did over the next week). I then asked him how he had lost two fingers from one of his hands. He laughed and explained that he was in his garden, digging with a spade during the war, when 'Boom!' The spade was knocked from his hand and there was blood. He had hit a landmine. He laughed again. I asked him what was so funny. He replied, "I laugh because they took only my fingers and missed the rest of me!"

During one weekend, Mr and Mrs B invited their other lodger and me to their part of the house for *kafer* (coffee). So, shoes off, in we went. More delicious home-made cherry fruit juice and stand-alone black coffee. This time, with my English-speaking fellow lodger, I got the chance to explain that, in England, I drink *voda* (water) and very little coffee, so avoided the numerous top-ups.

During our conversation, the student lawyer said the Serbs had killed his father and his aunt, who had been with his father at the time. They did not trust Milošević to keep his word about promises he may have made about Kosovo.

I explained that I would listen only and did not wish to intrude with questions about their past suffering. But the student said they wanted to talk and to explain what it was like during the recent war. "For example, have you seen a dead body in the street?"

"No, I have not."

"I have seen many and some in pieces," he explained.

We should be thankful and grateful that despite these horrors, they can still be grateful for what was done for them. They mentioned, especially, the help with food, clothing and water provided by Britain, America and the United Nation countries.

That afternoon, I felt the need to get some fresh air, exercise and a chance to think about what had been learned that morning. I went down the hill before turning right along a dusty road with allotments lining the edge of a pathway. A few biting midges decided to take to the air – they are not only found in Scotland. The area along the road was reminiscent of Kuwait, with ramshackle buildings interspersed with others under construction, with their clever timber roof structures, some of them opulent-looking. Vehicles travelled very fast and very frequently and there was evidence of the mud they splashed up in their wake over the plants adjacent to the road – all covered in clay-coloured dust. Peppers grew in one of the allotments. The plants were small bushes about fifteen inches high, quite spacial, which bear their red peppers at the same time as small white flowers.

Returning to the flat, I began reading the illustrated book, *Sarajevo – The Wounded City* by Miroslav Prstojevic, a journalist and native of the city. The city had 600,000 inhabitants before the war but, following the end of the war, it was not known how many remained. Of those that remained, many were maimed, their lives changed forever by evil acts that took just seconds.

One Saturday afternoon, while relaxing in the flat, I opened the side window in the kitchen and my attention was caught by two children playing outside in the glorious sunshine. Both were playing on swings: one in his balcony play area three storeys up and measuring about ten feet by four feet – his only play area; the other on the ground-floor patio. I watched them for some time, fascinated by their happy contentment with a simple toy that gave them pleasure and exercise simultaneously. Why were they content with their simple toys in quiet, tranquil surroundings? Meanwhile, back in the UK, many children of a similar age (five or six) demand attention, have short spans of contentment and moan about having nothing to do. The scene in front of me set me thinking – who has got it right? John Major, during his time as Prime Minister, advocated getting 'back to basics' while seemingly finding it difficult to explain what that actually meant or what it might entail. Maybe if he could have spent time in places with societies similar to the Bosnians, he might have found it helpful. I believed, at the time, that the scene of the two children playing happily on their swings, each unaware of the other, had given us a clue.

When visiting the city's hospital on my first visit – after we had been shepherded around the city to ensure we did not stray from the main streets and run the risk of detonating a landmine – I was shown onto a ward where an attractive young girl was lying in a bed. She was paralysed from the waist down, but smiled as if it was her birthday. She suffered pain from her back injury. I took her hand and did reflexology on it. The more I worked, the more she smiled, and I hope it helped a little. The story behind this tragedy was that she was out walking with a school friend when they came upon a small group of Serbian soldiers on a bridge, who gang-raped them before forcing them, at gunpoint, to jump over the parapet or be shot. Her friend died but she survived. The only cheerful thread to this dreadful story was that she was now engaged to be married. Her fiancé was on the ward when we visited.

In another private ward, a man of middle years was sat on the edge of his bed, staring into space, and rocking to and fro on his haunches all day long. I was told that, pre-war, he had been a very intelligent and successful qualified engineer. What a waste. What a sad existence.

All over the city, there were wounded people, but they do not show because they are hidden deeply in the mind, put there by horror, shock, trauma and, maybe, utter despair and disbelief. This is my interpretation based only upon what I perceived and was told and, in some instances, sensed or saw.

Fikreta's brother, Osma, invited me over for lunch at 2pm one day and asked if I had a favourite Bosnian dish. A leading question but, manners before mischief, I explained my lack of experience meant I had no favourite and that I had enjoyed all food while in Bosnia. I suspected peppers and yoghurt would feature prominently on the menu.

During our conversation over lunch, Osma said I could treat their home as my home. If I wished to visit at any time, all I had to do was telephone first to ensure someone in the family was at home. I thanked him and said I had not expected lunch nor to intrude upon their family life. He explained that I should not think that way because it was an old and genuine Bosnian custom to open the home and extend friendly, family hospitality without money having to be involved – as in the west. Now I felt embarrassed for my own country. I explained that large parts of Britain had once had this open-house attitude, but, sadly, it had largely disappeared. He thought this unfortunate because, as he said, "Money gets in the way of true friendship". A profound little sentence.

As a small gesture of thanks to Mr and Mrs Bosnia, I bought a small potted plant from the market and the opportunity to present it occurred when Mr B appeared at his door the following morning. I doubled back to the flat to get the plant. I had learnt by this time that Mrs B was very fond of flowering plants. On handing it over to them, it seemed that I 'lit the blue touchpaper'. There was much gesticulation and smiling, followed by going down the outside steps to knock on the door of Saban (pronounced Shaban – an Islamic name). He appeared and also invited for a celebratory *kafer*. He very kindly translated for me to explain to Mr and Mrs B that British people enjoy giving gifts as a 'thank you'. It did not represent payment in any way, but was a sign of grateful friendship and for their kindness towards me. The Foreign Office should be grateful for the PR!

My thank you to Fikreta's mother, Yasma, sister, Alma and brother, Osma, was to treat them to a first-class meal in a very pleasant Persian restaurant in Sarajevo. I am pleased to say that the food and wine were excellent and it made for a good evening.

During the whole of my last trip, the political scene was precarious because Milošević was making threatening and worrying noises regarding the situation in Kosovo. Latterly, I learned that he had been given a ten-day ultimatum to comply with some UN requirement, following the deployment of observers. The ultimatum ran out the day after I was due to return home. I was thankful, because we had been told very clearly from the outset to carry our passports at all times and to be prepared to leave at a moment's notice. Certainly, the UN troops were armed and that had not been prominent on earlier visits.

Two days before departure, I was at the medical centre in the afternoon. I was walking along the corridor when I was confronted, at the far end, by two helmeted and heavily armed soldiers, who were heading towards me at a fast march. *This is it then*, I thought, and expected the order to "Get out, now!". Instead, one of them said, "Do you speak English?" In the split second it took to reply, "Yes, how can I help?" The rehearsed thoughts flashed through my head, including anticipating a follow-up sentence of "We have to advise you…"

Nothing as dramatic. They wished to know if there was a toilet they could use. They had been out on manoeuvres all day and were in great need of drainage. They were German UN troops. One of the leading two men spoke excellent English (probably a territorial who worked at BMW!) and the other spoke as little English as I could speak Bosnian. They were swiftly followed by the rest of their troop in equally desperate need. The place was soon swarming with UN troops.

It gave me the opportunity to ask if they were allowed to tell me what was happening in Kosovo. They confirmed that 'slobber-chops' had until the next Monday to behave himself. If not, they, the German Army, would stay and, in the following thirty hours, the German Air Force and other NATO planes would fly in. I remained pleased to be leaving very soon.

My return journey home, or rather to London to speak at a national reflexology conference, was in two parts – Sarajevo to Ljubljana Airport and thence to Heathrow, London. There was a two-hour delay before the final flight to Heathrow and the time was passed largely by indulging a hobby – people-watching.

Have you noticed how seasoned travellers look 'seasoned'? They sit nonchalantly reading a magazine or newspaper in their own little bubble world; the businessmen are in their uniform of lounge suits and tie and pretend a suave demeanour. Power-dressed types pace about and respond to the urgent bidding of their mobile phones as if every millisecond cannot be missed while wandering about the place – perhaps that is why they are called mobile phones. Another lady of apparent confidence poses at the bar for reasons unknown but, while in my orbit, does not appear to have attracted any attention. What a shame.

Another lady recognises a friend and charges towards her enthusiastically – maybe it is a kind of magnetic attraction generated by wrist bangles and glistening necklaces, which were very evident on both individuals. This dubious pastime was brought to a halt by the broadcast boarding announcement for our flight homeward and the luxury of being among English-speaking people once again.

The flat I occupied during the final weeks (thanks to the kindness of Dr. Muftic), it is the top one, with some washing drying. Just the place to be for someone still not too secure at height, but with excellent views.

The devastated residential block opposite an unscathed football stadium. Note: the stairs remain intact. It was always said in WWII that it was the safest place to shelter.

With my colleague Mrs Linda Rumbles, trying to stay warm outside the old medical centre in Sarajevo. February 1998.

The house where I was looked after almost as one of the family. The wall-scars are from the war.

Dr Mirsad Muftic (3rd from right) – the Medical Officer of Health Sarajevo, and some of his Physiotherapists at the presentation of the I.I.R certificates. Frikreta, our interpreter, is 1st from left.

chapter six

The Enjoyment & Value of Sport

I have enjoyed sport from an early age without ever reaching an outstanding standard. With team games – cricket, hockey, rugby or soccer – I could simply be relied upon to attend and try one hundred per cent throughout the match. Although exhausting at times, it was always an enjoyable experience. Hockey at adult club level was with Westland Sports and as a guest player with Yeovil Hockey Club. The after-match drinks and socialising were usually just as much fun as the games themselves and provided an antidote to the pressures of everyday work and life.

Soccer-playing days were of a somewhat mixed level, from Westland Apprentice team in the Yeovil and District League, to training in the evenings on Yeovil Town's sloping pitch that no longer exists. They now have an excellent pitch and stadium, and graduated from the old Southern League to a pinnacle level of one season in the Football Championship before a gradual decline to non-league football, which is where they are at the time of writing this book.

The one unexpected glimpse of relative glory was to be accepted in Bristol Rovers' pre-season training, which, in 1952/53, was held annually on a sports complex in Weston-Super-Mare, Somerset. I was completely out of my depth. Rovers, at that time, were in the upper echelons of the old second division; the first division being the highest level prior to the advent of the Premier League. The pace at which they passed the ball and moved around the pitch during the practice sessions was, at times, mesmerising.

The training was organised and overseen by the late Bert Tann, an outstanding manager and tactician, renowned for developing players from schoolboy standard to league standard. He organised his team so that each player knew the part he should play and a number of set moves were rehearsed, particularly among the forwards. I remember the 'W formations' prominently, with every forward knowing their place in it so well that they did not have to look for their teammate. They knew where he would be and could move the ball among each other at speed. Rovers were frequently in the top six, but folded towards the end of the season.

It was an experience to be with such players as Geoff Bradford, who had just gained international recognition; Bill Roost, a no-nonsense centre half; Harry Bamford, a thoughtful and reliable defender at right back (tragically killed in a road accident); Ron Nicholls, goalkeeper and Gloucester County cricketer; and Barrie Meyer, centre-forward and county cricketer who later became a test match umpire.

A remarkable player was left-winger Peter Hooper, who had one of the hardest shots in soccer in the days of the leather ball. He was slightly built, about 5 ft 6, and had very small feet, almost like hooves! These attributes, combined with a very high in-step with which to kick a ball correctly, made him a force to be reckoned with and was the cause of him scoring many goals throughout his playing career.

The club promised to follow me in any games on returning home, but I heard nothing, which was not a surprise because it had not been possible to step up to the standard of a club in the second division. A couple of years later, hockey became my winter game.

We had a good hockey club at Westland Aircraft, with excellent facilities. As a schoolboy, I had played the game in the spring term, after rugby in the autumn. Strangely, I became involved with hockey when an old school friend phoned me and asked if I could help because they were short for the game on the following Saturday. Seven seasons later, I was still in the team. Our highlight was going through one whole season of twenty-four games unbeaten. It was a joy to play in midfield in front of my long-time friend and ex-school mate, Rex Beable, whom I remember to this day. We kept in touch until cancer overcame him when we were both in our seventies.

Probably the most exciting experience regarding soccer was not as a player but as a spectator. It was in 1948/49, when Yeovil Town, then in the Southern League, had a famous run in the FA Cup. The highlight was on 29th January 1949 when they beat first-division Sunderland 2–1 after extra time, in front of a crowd of over 17,000.

To set the scene, it is necessary to recall that my

family were regular supporters. We used to gather at my grandmother's house, 133 Huish, prior to all home matches. Her house was about four hundred yards along the same road from which the ground was named. The gathering was made up of my grandmother, mother, an aunt and an uncle. My father was not a sports type, but became a supporter much later in life having been worn down by the enthusiasm of the rest of the family.

This family group would walk the short distance to the ground. We had our regular spot near one of the goals and I was put at the front. This was my introduction to semi-professional soccer from the age of around five. Our chosen spot gave us an excellent view of any goalmouth action and caused me to become fascinated by goalkeeping. I put it into practice in my late teens before converting to midfield because my growth had stopped at 5 ft 9 – too short for playing in goal at a reasonable standard.

Spectators stood on old railway sleepers, laid end-to-end on an earth bank to form the steps of the terracing. There was a small grandstand and one covered end; otherwise, you took your chance with the elements.

It was against this background of regular support that the scene was set for the Sunderland match. The occasion was dramatic because Yeovil's regular and excellent goalkeeper, Stan Hall, was injured on the Thursday before the game and had to be replaced by Dickie Dyke, who had played in the first team only once and was in his early twenties.

The home team were all part-time professionals with day jobs, which meant they trained two or three times a week in the evenings – often in the dark, as this was before floodlights. Any work at the ground was under the brightest light that could be mustered and fixed to the roof of the dressing room, which was in one corner of the ground. Because of their exploits in the previous third round of the cup, when they beat second-division Bury 3–1, most of their employers gave the players the week off so that they could train full-time for the Sunderland game.

The team was led by player/manager Alec Stock. Yeovil was his first club immediately after leaving the army with the rank of major. His ability to lead men became evident. In the fortnight before the game, I was outside my grandmother's house one evening and saw the squad running along the street in the dark. In among the complete squad of players and setting the pace was the manager. The team was in the lower half of the league table, but he was beginning to improve things and, when it came to the cup games, they all produced a far higher performance. It was like watching a different team, quite amazing.

All of this was in great contrast to Sunderland Soccer Club, who played at Roker Park with the facilities associated with a team in the old first division and awash with too much money. In 1948/49, Sunderland reputedly had the most valuable forward line at approximately £55,000. They had signed the famous Len Shackleton for a reported £20,000 and were known as 'The Bank of England'. This was what Yeovil's part-timers were up against and it was not surprising that the sports journalists gave them no chance of beating league opposition twice. Once was a fluke, they suggested.

The press made much of the sloping pitch at Huish. It had an excellent playing surface but sloped from side to side with about a 6 ft drop from one wing-line to the other. The only difficulty found on it, when playing some years later, was that the higher wing area waved up and down like a mini roller coaster, which made ball control difficult when running fast or weaving around an opponent.

A great deal of work was necessary to prepare for the large crowd. The usual attendance was 3,000–4,000 with perhaps 8,000 at particularly attractive fixtures. Extra terracing and temporary seating was erected and every available space filled. The temporary seating placed some spectators almost on the wings of the pitch. It was a new experience for the visiting players. The actual attendance was recorded at 17,123 but it was claimed some non-ticket holders took it to over 18,000 tightly packed in. It was quite a sight to be seen and some adventurous spectators were perched high up on some surrounding trees.

The expectation and excitement built up, like a pressure cooker that exploded at the 2pm kick-off (this was to allow for the possibility of poor light conditions towards the end of the ninety minutes). Yeovil took the lead in the 28th minute, when Alec Stock took a through pass, swivelled round and shot into the top corner of the net past Sunderland goalkeeper, John Mapson. Supporters could hardly believe what was unfolding before their eyes.

It remained 1–0 at half-time. But Yeovil's goalkeeper made a mistake that allowed Sunderland to equalise early in the second half. It seemed that this goal would burst the bubble and Sunderland would go on to win the match. However, to our amazement, 1–1 remained the score at full-time, resulting in thirty minutes of extra time.

Under normal circumstances, there would have been a

replay at Roker Park. But during the early post-war period, when the FA Cup competition restarted, extra time was used because of travel restrictions caused by fuel shortages.

There was an unforeseen scare for the home supporters when fog descended at the start of extra time. It almost forced the match to be abandoned. Fortunately, it drifted away as quickly as it had come down, the fading light adding to the drama of the occasion.

Fifteen minutes into extra time, Yeovil's centre forward, Eric Bryant, ran onto a through pass and raced towards the Sunderland goal as their keeper came off his line towards him, and their centre-half Stan Hall chased back. As the three of them came together, Bryant managed to prod the ball goal-wards into an unguarded net. The time it took to roll all the way into the goal seemed more like minutes than seconds. Pandemonium broke out; the home supporters must have been heard throughout Somerset.

2–1 but still fifteen minutes to go. Time enough for a team of Sunderland's quality to upset the apple cart, particularly as their full-time training over the part-timers was beginning to show. As soon as the referee blew the final whistle, the crowd burst onto and all over the pitch, shouting, jumping, running, waving their green-and-white scarves and generally enjoying the moment.

What a game; what a day. There had just been enough daylight to complete the game and a headline in one of the Sunday papers the next morning read: 'Yeovil Bury Sunderland'.

For the fifth round game away to Manchester United, a whole train load, including our family group, travelled north along with numerous other coaches. The town was deserted. The game was played at Maine Road, Manchester – the City ground. United's Old Trafford ground had been bombed in 1941 and had not yet been restored. A crowd of 81,565 was recorded, of which 6,000 were estimated to be from Yeovil.

We made sure that, for such a great game, we had seats in the grandstand and we looked across the ground to the huge open-air terrace that was packed to capacity. I will always remember the sight of children being passed overhead from the top of the terrace down to the front like a human waterfall. There is nothing to beat the generous, friendly spirit of Mancunians. After the match, as we wandered around Piccadilly still wearing our green-and-white scarves, strangers came up to us and praised the sporting manner in which our team had played and never gave up, despite being outplayed. Sadly, this behaviour has long been missing from the game.

Money has replaced manners. Even the FA Cup itself has been devalued by leading clubs fielding weak teams to save their first-choice players for the lucrative European Cup or for premiership games. The FA has let this happen when it might have upheld its famous competition by ruling that all participants must field their strongest team, under penalty of dismissal from the competition for the following season. Culprits would have to be hit in the pocket to make them take notice. Where has the pride of playing in the FA Cup gone? It lingers with the lesser clubs, who can make a name for themselves and their town or city with a good cup run.

To the game itself, it was such a shame to see a below-par performance by Yeovil. Whereas they had played way above their league performance in the previous rounds, they seemed to be overcome by one of the greatest managers in my lifetime, Matt Busby. He was in the process of assembling his first great United side.

Within the first twenty minutes, Yeovil conceded a soft goal from a corner when their keeper froze as a weak header crept into the corner of his goal. He watched but remained stuck to the spot. It seemed to demoralise the side and a little later he suffered a gash to his stomach when diving at the feet of Jack Rowley, as he scored United's third goal. Bravely, he somehow managed to last the ninety minutes. But it was a further setback for Yeovil and certainly very painful for him to have an uncharacteristically poor game.

This is to take nothing away from United, who played some excellent soccer. Among the eight they scored was the best goal I have ever seen. In one fluent move, the ball reached Charlie Mitten out on the left touchline. He ran forward a few yards before hitting a low, fast, pass to Jack Rowley to run onto. From about twenty yards out, he hit it left-footed on the volley into the corner of the net. The amazing thing was that from the time the ball left Mitten, it travelled off the ground and remained level until it hit the back of the net. Magnificent. That was the measure of skill with which United played throughout and they thoroughly deserved to win, but maybe not 8–0! For the record, they were beaten by Wolverhampton Wanderers in the final.

My enthusiasm for soccer has declined as money and fooling the referee (i.e. diving or exaggerating a minor tackle or collision to get an opponent booked or sent off the pitch) is seen too often. How strange that managers of the offending players never see it. They should be told to pay attention or visit Specsavers!

Some of the decline in the quality of games has occurred since the founding of the Premiership, due to reasons including the ridiculous impatience and egos of club directors and, latterly, owners; the power of TV companies, which dictate kick-off times to suit schedules but not supporters; and the fact that too many games are played within congested competitions at the expense of the well-being of the players upon whom the whole enterprise depends.

Referring to less glamorous pastimes, another sport I enjoyed was small-bore rifle shooting at the 11th Gloucester's indoor rifle range. This occupied one evening a week in my thirties until the amount of travelling with work made it impossible to continue.

Golf has proved an excellent pastime and social life. As a member of two clubs in turn and captain for a year at one of them, it has been the scene of some very pleasant experiences. At Clevedon Golf Club, a number of monthly medals were won, plus one cup for which I never received a miniature due to 'an administrative lapse'.

Tickenham Golf Club was a much more gratifying experience. It was only a nine-hole course but was quite challenging. A number of low-handicap visiting players were deceived by its variations. Again, monthly medals were gratefully received and there were two highlights, both unexpected, which are detailed below.

One pleasant Saturday morning, I set out with my playing partner in a regional competition in which a number of clubs hosted a round of golf. The winner then went on to a regional event and, ultimately, to the final. It was sponsored by the golf ball manufacturer Titleist in association with Footjoy. On offer was a dozen of their latest golf balls to anyone who managed a hole-in-one. The occasion was the 'Hall of Fame Golf Championship Day'.

To my utter delight, a hole-in-one was achieved on the 195-yard third hole. My partner shouted out that the ball had scuttled across the green and disappeared down the hole. Neither of us really believed it until we reached the green. I was on such a high that I took eleven on the next dog-leg hole, hitting the first three efforts off the tee into the woods that ran along one side of the fairway. This brought me back down to earth, knowing the chance of winning our club entry had disappeared among the trees. I have a framed metal certificate on the study wall from the Hole-in-One Golf Society, a commemorative tie, a gold bag tag and, long ago, a dozen brand-new Titleist golf balls. It was a pleasure to follow tradition and buy everyone a drink when back in the clubhouse and as other players came back after their morning game.

The second highlight of being a member of Tickenham was to be invited by the club professional, Tony Mealing, to be one of a team of four players he intended to enter into the Arizona World Pro-Am 2000 Tournament Golf Links. The tournament was sponsored by Bollé and the Golf Rules Dictionary. Our complete team included professional Tony Mealing, Andrew Shimmen (team captain) and Sir John Hunt, a resident player who kindly joined us out there as one of our number was unavailable at the last minute.

The whole experience was completely new to me and, at times, confusing. For example, we signed in on the first morning and when I turned to pick up my clubs, they were nowhere to be seen. Panic was quickly followed by embarrassment when a courteous attendant explained they had been loaded onto our buggy, which carried our team identification flag. The Americans rarely walk anywhere.

The tournament ran for four days under February's clear blue skies. Playing in high temperatures, we completed eighteen holes per day. During the four games, there was one scary moment and one memorable embarrassment.

The scary moment was when hitting a satisfying long shot up the fairway and into a gully. Fortunately, Andrew Shimmen, a South African, was walking alongside where the ball landed. It was easily visible, so I went to go into the slight gully to play it, when Andrew put a restraining hand on my shoulder, said nothing, but pointed to quite a large snake. It matched its surroundings so well I had not seen it. Luckily Andrew's keen eye and familiarity with similar scenes back home had come to the fore. The golf ball was left in the gully and a new one played from the nearest point under penalty of one shot and with simultaneous great relief.

The embarrassing moment occurred at the first tee at the start of one of our games. It must be emphasised that back home, we were only ever accompanied by our partner, who marked our card. It was nearly always just the two of us. Occasionally, there might be a few members milling about but no other audience. Here, it was the full works, where you were announced on the tee in the same way as shown in the televised competitions. There was added tension as the announcer picked up the microphone and said, "On the first tee is Adrian Seager of Tickenham (with emphasis on the 'ham') Golf Club, UK." I hit the ball all of ten to fifteen yards and had to stand aside while the other three people hit off the tee properly. Throughout my waiting, I never took my eyes off the wretched ball – never have I focused so hard for so long. When hitting my second shot, it was creamed straight down the fairway. Embarrassment over, confidence and normality restored.

We were all given new waterproof golf jackets with the name of the tournament on the front, a ping putter engraved with the name of the competition, and a pair of wraparound sunglasses from the sponsor Bollé. Unfamiliar perks indeed; it made you feel as if you had arrived on a whole new level.

I will always remember the beauty and quality of the practice putting greens at each of our four host clubs. They could have been entries at the Chelsea Flower Show.

The prizes, based upon the gross score of each team over the completed four rounds of golf, were made at the concluding dinner and ceremony. To our surprise, there was a joke prize for 'the worst drive of the competition'. We each thought it was heading my way. Instead, it was 'won' by one of the German players for hitting a trashcan (i.e. dustbin) situated by one of the tees. Phew! Now to relax and enjoy the whole scene, with good wine, a few jokes and excellent companions and acquaintances of the night, in the best possible sense.

Regarding sport generally, my interest in the past year has extended to part-ownership of seven horses, who are in training with some well-known, established, successful trainers. This has been possible by joining the Owners' Group. We buy a small share in a horse and have the choice of renewing them annually. It's a small outlay and we are kept informed about our horses via a monthly magazine of excellent quality and by regular emails and videos.

The sport I enjoy as a spectator and 'investor' is horse racing. The horses always do their best. Although, on a very few occasions, the chosen horse will not race. They have a mind of their own and every trainer will tell you that if they are not right mentally on the day, they will not perform. I prefer National Hunt meetings over flat racing. It's not simply the challenge of the jumps, it's more the atmosphere of places like Cheltenham and Worcester – where I had membership before we moved across the country to Lincolnshire.

After deciding some years ago that racing provided a fascinating opportunity of an interest that could provide a return, I began to invest . Naturally, the return is variable, but a bank has been built up enough to overcome lean spells when selections have not gone my way. As with life, what we get from it is in proportion to the effort made. I keep detailed records and make disciplined selections, taking account of information gleaned and recorded: the going; the trainer; his winning streak. I am not giving away any more hints, but one small perk is that returns are tax-free – a rarity these days and long may it be allowed to continue.

In summary, sport is good for you and a nose broken twice, a big toe broken twice – once by a horse standing on it – and some broken ribs are a minor legacy. Many top players suffer arthritis or some other condition that limits mobility later in their lives and they deserve support in a way similar to that provided by the Injured Jockeys Fund and Racing Welfare.

Non-League Yeovil beat Bury 3—1. Here is their line-up. Left to right (standing): R. Davies, R. Keeton, A. Hickman, S. Hall, I. Blizzard, R. Wright; (sitting: F. Hamilton, A. Stock, F. Bryant, N. Collins, J. Hargreaves.

The Yeovil town team that reached the 5th round of the F.A. Cup, Feb 1949

A rare day when Clevedon Golf Club, Somerset, hosted a sponsored ladies'
professional Pro-Am. tournament, 19th July 1989. Left to right: Paul Elwood,
Frank Skuse, Jo Foreman (visiting U.S professional), Fred Hyde, myself (caddy
to Jo – lucky me). Sadly Fred Hyde died suddenly just before a club competition
on19th July 1997, aged 66 – A sad loss of a past captain and popular member

Another rare occasion at Clevedon Golf
Club. I actually won the cup I'm holding.

Pine course – by dreaded water.
Note the suburb condition of the course.

Arizona World Pro-Am 2000, Tickenham Golf Club Team.
Left to right: Lord John Hunt (guest member) (25); Andrew Shimmen (9);
Tony Mealing, Tickenham G.C Assistant Pr

Left to right: Lord John Hunt (guest member) (25); Andrew Shimmen (9);
myself (21)

chapter seven

Media Moments

I suppose my first experience of facing the TV cameras came as early as 1963, aged twenty-nine, at Garnett College, London University (now known as the University of Greenwich). It occurred at the end of the full-time training course for those who aspired to teach in secondary and further education. The engineers selected a panel of six to face an invited audience from the public. They chose me to be chairman, which involved introducing my colleagues on the panel and directing the questions from the audience to an appropriate colleague. Discussion or argument often needed a degree of courteous control. The whole event was televised, recorded and reviewed. It was similar to the BBC's *Question Time*, without the chairman involving himself in the debate or interrupting with smart comments from a script.

During my time as Vice President, UK, of the IIR, I received a telephone call from the Chairman of the Institute of Complimentary Medicine asking me to represent that organisation in a BBC TV West News item that evening, in the company of the chief medical officer of health for that region. That was my one-and-only appearance on live TV, in which it was easy to ignore the camera by concentrating upon the attractive presenter.

It was amazing the number of people who contacted me afterwards to say, "I saw you on TV last night." Thankfully, no comment was made about content.

It illustrated the power of television and, more widely, the discipline needed for documentary programmes to be factual and unbiased. The media has a great responsibility to maintain the discipline of the early head of the BBC, the late Lord Reith; namely, to inform, educate and entertain. The modern media appears to stray away from that formula at times; perhaps it has allowed itself to broadcast the wishes of that shadowy group of the rich and powerful at the expense of balance?

As retirement came into my mind gradually and persistently, it seemed fun to explore the possibility of becoming a film or TV extra. This episode had a brief and exciting flight before crash-landing among the fickle world of the broadcasting media generally. If ever 'being in the right place at the right time' plays a part, this is it.

Zen Directories Castings Limited placed a small advertisement in our daily newspaper inviting us to attend 'a one-day confidence course for television and film extras'. The fee was £25, the venue was London, and the temptation too great. On a sunny morning in June 2007, I set off from Pershore Station at 7.42am, heading for Paddington. What was not in the plan was a delay at Didcot Junction because of the all-too-familiar 'fault on the line'. This resulted in me arriving later than anticipated for the big day.

Having found the venue, just a few minutes before the schedule start-time of 11am, I opened the door to be confronted by a large room full of people making a large collective noise, like schoolchildren before the first lesson of the day. Queen Bee, Amanda, soon had us organised and our personal details and facial photographs filed away.

The first challenge was to study and remember a script of an advert and then, in turn, to face the TV camera and present the content. It read as follows:

"Do you get tired of pressing buttons and getting options? I know I do. But now I have discovered X Ltd Direct. X Ltd Direct can solve your problems, of whatever kind, twenty-four hours a day. Give them a call on 07800-- ----. You will speak to a real person!"

The name of the fictitious company and the telephone number has been omitted from the script because of similarity with a well-known company. The content of this mock advertisement was easy to present with feeling because it represented a frustration that was as common then, in 2007, as it remains today. Thankfully, my effort was well received. If I had been a dog at Crufts, it might have got a 'Highly Commended'!

Then followed a robbery scene, a pub fracas caused when a group of smokers were asked to extinguish their cigarettes. All did except one, who turned nasty. Eventually, 'nasty man' is arrested by a policeman (I enjoyed that bit – pity there was no uniform or truncheon).

The remainder of the morning session was occupied with role-playing a scene where one of the characters had misplaced his mobile phone and caused chaos looking for it. It was a scene all too familiar to my domestic life. The whole day was conducted in a bit of a daze and closed with a crowd scene for all of us at the races – requiring mixed emotions for winners and losers, before finishing at 6pm.

The next day at 8am, Amanda telephoned to invite me to a Channel 4 TV casting that evening. I refused because it was not possible to postpone a number of appointments at short notice. It was fortunate, because the following Monday I learned the casting had been cancelled at the last minute. Not unusual, apparently.

Two weeks later, Zen Directories Castings Ltd got me a casting appointment for a British Airways commercial. I attended, wearing a lounge suit, as requested, to look like a businessman. The role was about a careless steward spilling coffee on my lap and the consequent scene around the mishap. It was a rather strange experience. The shoot was scheduled for two weeks after the casting meeting. It was not a surprise to hear no more from the film company.

There was one more invite, from a different studio, to cast for a Terry's Chocolate advertisement, but the date clashed with attendance at the Association of Reflexologists Annual Conference at Warwick University, where my book, *Reflexology and Associated Aspects of Health*, was displayed and on sale.

I had a further glimpse into the world of television when I attended media training studios, based at that time in Nottingham. It involved travel from home to Nottingham one day a week for a period of time. I received training in presenting to camera, reading from an autocue and voice training. The latter, with Jan Cox, included breathing exercises (to be practised at home, as well as the one-to-one on-site training). A very interesting aspect of this was to demonstrate my voice range, from highest to lowest and back to highest. Apparently, I had seven stages involving pace, variation and breathing. We spent over an hour to improve the breathing – a new and fascinating experience.

The company spent time producing videos of my efforts and these were to be available on the open market for producers and/or agents to view. They had a casting directory and, for a fee, you could be included in it for a year, with a review at the year-end. Unfortunately, there was no link or placement with an agency or with a prospective agent. It was pot luck if anyone thought I might be useful. No one did. I continued life as before, but was prepared for anything that might come my way. Nothing did come my way.

Instead, I got a broadcasting job by having the nerve – boosted by a somewhat liquid lunch – to walk into the BBC Radio Bristol offices and ask for an audition. The polite lady at reception explained I could not do that, but she would take my details and forward them to the sports director, as I had said my potential first choice would be in sports broadcasting. I assumed that would be the last I heard of it – a typical 'don't call us, we will call you'. Not so! The following day, I was invited back at 5pm to meet the manager of Radio Bristol, the CEO himself.

At that meeting, he said, "If a studio is available, I would like to record your voice." Fortunately, one was free and we made our way to it. It was at this point of no return that nerves were beginning to play a part. He said, "I want you to speak for one minute on any subject of your choice." The only topic that came to mind in the short time available was Bristol City's football match last Saturday in the second division. I asked for a few minutes to gather my thoughts – there was no time to write bullet points on a card.

My eventual one-minute summary was very jerky and disappointing, I thought. Yet, to my utter surprise, he did not criticise but said that I had a storytelling voice and he would contact me in due course.

Yet more surprise! I received an invitation a couple of days later from the sports producer, David Solomons, to come into the BBC studio the following Saturday to sit in and experience the live programme of linked reports coming in all afternoon. He thought the experience would give a good foundation and introduction to the programme. It certainly was hectic and he was excellent in linking everything into a coherent presentation for the public.

My first assignment as a freelance sports reporter was with BBC Radio Bristol in November 1979. One Thursday, I was told to go to Bath City FC on the following Saturday to cover their home match. It was suggested that it would be helpful to link up with a studio engineer to be briefed on using the portable equipment I would be using. This was an understatement. He was very helpful, and notes and sketches were made as he outlined what was involved.

The schedule of the broadcast would take the standard format. This was a two-minute introduction before kick-off to outline and name the players involved, then thirty-second updates every fifteen minutes, unless there was a goal scored, when the producer in the studio must be told. There would be a two-minute half-time summary and a final summary at full-time, again lasting two minutes. These times were critical. Apparently, it was related to the contract for local radio. If the times were abused, the station could lose the licence to broadcast local sport.

I set off to a ground I hadn't visited before, with equipment never used before and with the need to provide sufficient time to purchase a pocket stopwatch. The personal drama did not stop there. After the game, the Bath City manager had agreed to an interview. It would be completely unscripted and I had to trust that he would appear in the press box before the producer (back at base) was ready and gave me the signal 'Go' into my headphones.

He duly appeared on time but, before we could get started, his opening words were: "If he's here, I'm not doing this." 'He' was the reporter from the local paper. My instinctive and immediate reaction was to turn to this person and, in my best imitation of a sergeant major, say, "Get out, now." His expression was as open-mouthed as a freshly landed salmon. To my relief, he did not argue, but left the press box immediately. The interview started on cue and went well. The voice training did come in useful, after all!

As I disconnected from the press box and was packing the microphone and equipment away, it occurred to me that it would be wise to have a word with the fleeing reporter. After all, we were, in a sense, part of the same media. He accepted my apology for rudeness and went on to explain that he and the manager had fallen out during the week before this match and were not on speaking terms. First lesson learned: get to the venue in good time to get 'the feel' of the place and not simply where the press box and other essential facilities are located.

There were lighter moments within my five-year stint as a reporter. How busy you are is in direct proportion to the producer's opinion of your capability. Three different producers were in post during my time at Radio Bristol. One had a thing about the phrase 'from end to end'. He regarded it as a taboo cliché. In an FA Cup game, it was so frantic at one stage that the ball was pinging about like a ball on a bagatelle board and I could not describe it more accurately than 'from end to end'. For the next minute after my two-minute stint, I got a fierce reprimand in my headphones (which are worn at all times to maintain contact with the studio).

Another producer assigned me to report on Yeovil Town's games, home and away. There was one game away at Frickley Town in a Southern League fixture that lingers in the mind.

We got off the coach and went to the changing rooms beneath the main grandstand. In fact, it was the only grandstand and contained the press box, which looked out upon a huge coal stack at the far side of the pitch, making it very clear that we were in mining country. This was emphasised further when I went down to the Yeovil changing room to get the team news. On opening the door, a cloud of smoke billowed out and the players could not be seen. They were busy coughing as they were getting changed into their kit. There was much laughter when one of the players claimed it was a plot to handicap the away team. The culprit was an inefficient chimney to an open-coal fire. It was a cold weather winter fixture and the players quickly realised the luxury of choice: to keep warm and choke or change in the corridor and freeze. They chose the latter and the opportunity of acclimatising to the outside temperature as soon as possible.

There were other hazards to add to the growing off-field pantomime. There was no telephone line to the press box and, therefore, no direct link from me to the studio. Instead, I had to leave the press box and go down a flight of stairs to a telephone point to tell the studio any news. I would do this approximately every fifteen minutes. I'd also have to hope to hear it ring, if and when they wanted to contact me. A lot can happen in a match while dialling a fairly long number.

Because it was midwinter, I needed light. When I asked the adjacent local newspaper reporter to switch on the light, he said, "There isn't one."

"What do you mean?" I asked.

"It's above your head," he replied.

It was, but vandals had stolen the light bulb. So I was in the dark, trying to make my notes, while running up and downstairs every time something exciting happened. When it was time for the reports towards the end of the game, I had to ask the newspaper reporter to tell me if anything significant had happened while I was busy downstairs telephoning the studio. *Match of the* Day reporters do not know the half of it!

Another off-the-record occurrence happened at Maidenhead, where, at the time of Yeovil's visit, the facilities for the press were somewhat limited and, in an unguarded moment, I mentioned this shortcoming. This resulted in the host chairman approaching me with a severe reprimand. Full marks to him for defending his club's reputation and a fitting reminder for me to stick to the game.

On an appreciative note, there was the opportunity to meet and interview some well-known figures of the 1980s. The late Malcolm Alison of Manchester City and media fame. Barry Fry, when he was the manager at Barnet in the Southern League – a jovial character and popular with TV and radio. He was an interesting man to interview and was later involved in the administrative side of the game. Laurie McNeminie was manager of Southampton when Kevin Keegan was in his team. We met, briefly, when he was the main speaker at the launch of the Great Mills Western League. He kindly granted me a few minutes after the ceremony.

There was also the opportunity of working on one-off assignments for other radio stations and these included Radio Sheffield, Radio Nottingham, Radio Derby and others. It made sense to use a local reporter than to send someone to a game in the Bristol area. The matches concerned were all in the evening and all against Bristol Rovers. Naturally, you had to concentrate on the visiting away team and ensure you identified their players correctly and with appropriate emphasis.

I recall one horror game when Bristol Rovers were at home at their Eastville Stadium (later an IKEA store!) on a dreadfully wet evening and on an equally soggy pitch. The visitors had a Czechoslovakian goalkeeper and I made a hash of pronouncing his name and compounded my error when attempting to say that the game was being played in stamina-sapping conditions; I got the words muddled and was rescued by the programme producer, over the headphones, saying, "Stop, take a breath, slow down and go again." It was as bad as 'dying on stage'.

Towards the end of another game at Bath City, I made my two-minute report about fifteen minutes before the end of the game. At the end of the brief stint, through my headphones, the producer said a line had gone down and I was to switch immediately to live commentary until the end of the game. This was an enjoyable gift and lead to me being chosen to share commentary with Johnathon Pearce at Wembley for the final of FA Vase in May 1982.

Johnathon went on to work for the national network and became a regular contributor on BBC's *Match of the Day* – congratulations to him. In contrast, I had to leave local radio because all my 'free time' was taken with the growing chiropody and reflexology practice and with teaching reflexology while holding down a full-time job prior to the imminent resignation from industry. So, there was insufficient time to continue radio broadcasting.

Throughout my radio work, there was always a kind welcome extended by the staff of the clubs and teams involved during my five-year contribution. When travelling with Yeovil, they always included me in the pre-match lunch and refused to let me pay. These and similar courtesies made the whole experience a joy.

Much later, I had the opportunity of being on the receiving end of a BBC Radio Bristol interview, as a small part of one of their excellent morning programmes. It was hosted by Chris Searle, who was a well-known TV broadcaster at the time and a very well-respected and courteous interviewer. My reason for the interview, plus a question-and-answer session, was the publication of my first book, Two Feet from Our Thoughts – an attempt to persuade people to value the part our feet play in our overall health and mobility.

It was a pleasant opportunity and I took the chance of writing a few bullet points on a card beforehand. These would help me make sure key items would be included as the interview and the question-and-answer session progressed. This was the value of a little experience of similar situations. It meant that the interviewer did not govern the entire session nor the pace at which it was presented.

Preparation before any interview or important meeting is something I have found useful over the years. They can be nervous occasions; we can leave a meeting and only then, when we have relaxed, do we realise we failed to mention one or two key points. These little hiccups can turn an opportunity to impress into a failure. Conversely, a little preparation can bring joyous success.

chapter eight

Observations & Optimism

It has taken longer than intended to complete this book. A determined positive attitude has made it awkward to look backwards and it is this mismatch that has made recording my life more difficult than imagined. Yet, with the loving help of my wife, Norma, and our family, it has been achieved. My sincere thanks for their help and encouragement and this is in addition to earlier thanks recorded in the acknowledgement section. However, it is time to make some overall observations.

During the last eighty years, life in England has changed; from open-door friendliness in the late 1930s to the need for locked doors, alarm systems and cyber security where and when possible. During this time, trust has diminished. Once a handshake was sufficient to confirm a deal. Now, it requires contracts and the involvement of lawyers from the outset. The mistrust of officialdom in all its forms has become widespread. This trend is not simply about money or the lack of it; it is about the general standard of behaviour and the need for caring action coupled with common sense.

Life used to be at a slower pace. Post offices were often local and you could get a paper driving license certificate over the counter, or a radio or television license. Modest savings could be deposited without any fuss. Now, we are lucky to have a post office. Many have gone because services were taken from them – a strange action by successive governments. We live in an age where sensible priorities in our everyday lives have been distorted. Cutting costs has long been the dogma of government, which continues to waste money.

For many years, our nation has displayed a disappointing characteristic. It is a failure by government of whatever party to listen to the people. The ability of individual members of parliament to represent the views of their constituents accurately can be thwarted by the party whips. This leaves the only direct link between parliament and the people as the cross on the ballot box paper of a general election. The exception was the referendum on whether to remain in or leave the European Union.

The leave result surprised the powers-that-be, who were completely unprepared for it. Perhaps some should have had counselling to help them deal with the shock. Nevertheless, we have a duty to vote because it was not long ago that many of us did not have that opportunity. If we cannot bother to take part, we are in no position to complain about the government we get.

It is a shame that we suffer national inertia at times. Witness the time it has taken to improve our railway system to a standard comparable to that enjoyed in other countries, such as Switzerland.

The need for more houses has existed since World War II and continues. We do not have enough affordable accommodation to match the needs of our growing population (it was fifty million in my school days). This imbalance between supply and demand has driven up house prices during this period of time. The situation is exaggerated by the increasing number of people who come to live and work in Britain, because it is wonderful country in which to live. We continue to build in brick when other countries, notably Germany, have factories producing house-packs with great precision, ready to be assembled on-site.

My wife and I were lucky to avoid some of these obstacles when I got a teaching post in Devon in 1962. We managed to gather money for a deposit on a mortgage for a small bungalow. Fortunately, my salary was sufficient to meet the mortgage repayment agreement. Our budget was tight and eating out, for example, was out of the question and not as popular in the 1960s – going to a restaurant was reserved for birthdays. Overseas holidays were what other people did. We did not have a television for over three years and then it was a second-hand black-and-white set from a helpful local shop. We saved to buy a washing machine – a luxury that helped to wash clothes at a speed that kept pace with the rate that our children made them dirty. It was normal for them to be mud-splattered because they were outside (voluntarily) most of the time, free to roam in the nearby fields and woodland. Sadly, this isn't always possible for many children today.

The only borrowing was for the purchase of a second-hand car, bought from a reputable local family business with a bank loan. This was arranged during a personal meeting with the manager of a well-known bank, who first clarified and discussed my salary and financial commitments, which he took into account when drawing up a written agreement for the duration of a personal loan and the monthly repayments by direct debit. This meeting took place in a friendly atmosphere and lasted no more than an hour. Today, you would be lucky to still have a local bank branch.

Reflecting upon the wider aspects of life, there seems to have been a decline in discipline generally – one reason why teaching is not as attractive as it used to be. Large gatherings occasionally turn riotous, which rarely used to happen. There is no denying the poor behaviour of some soccer crowds. In my boyhood and teens, attending a soccer match was a pleasure and a social event. Supporters were not segregated and enjoyed frequent banter among themselves. There was no need for crowd control stewards and never any throwing of objects onto the pitch. We stood shoulder to shoulder on the terraces and enjoyed the witticisms of some outspoken joker – usually aimed at the officials. It was all in good fun and rarely of a spiteful or vicious nature.

I believe that the decline in discipline stems from the emphasis put upon the reasons why miscreants behave the way they do, at the expense of increasing the need for self-discipline and having responsibility for our actions. There are few ultimate deterrents applied when the law is broken. Some judges hand out sentences so feeble that they bring the law itself into disrepute. In such cases, the police officers responsible for apprehending the offender must despair.

Disrespect for the law is dangerous and it may be time for many aspects of the operation to be reviewed. Political correctness has, on occasions, proved frustrating and contrary to common sense. It, too, requires critical review, to avoid our language being distorted into an incoherent muddle and confusion.

This contrasts to life in Britain after World War II, when there was respect for the law and for the police. In those days, there was a police station in every town and many villages had a police house for the local constable, who had a good idea of what was going on in his area and would often keep order simply by 'having a word' with any suspect individual. The age of bobbies-in-cars came later. Police stations had the facilities to detain rascals, looked after by those on night duty. This provided safety for the public and a bed for the miscreant. Members of the public could go to their local station to report an incident by talking to a duty officer. This may seem trivial but it minimised misunderstanding and poor communication. Today, there is little personal contact between police and the public except after an incident or accident has happened.

How strange that centralisation, coupled with impersonal computerised accounts, is seen as progress by some and normal by others. This 'progress' has been made alongside a trend of decreasing personal contact and communication, so vital for any form of mental tranquillity. In my teens, doctor's surgeries, for example, were numerous and local. Today, they are scarce, far less face-to-face and have overcrowded waiting areas with electronic screens that show the name of the next patient invited to see the doctor, who, having welcomed you, will swivel round to stare at their computer screen.

There was a time in the 1950s and 1960s when a surgery would be found in a large family house and run by a senior partner, nurses and receptionists (these would often be retired nurses). They managed their own team rota so that there was always a doctor on call seven days a week, twenty-four hours a day. You could call the surgery any time and speak to either your own doctor or the one on duty.

One of my earliest reflections is of the war years, 1939 to 1945. It was a period in which there was fear throughout the country. The fear of being bombed and of loved ones being killed, coupled with the fact that, as individuals, we could do nothing to stop it. There are parallels to be drawn with the Covid-19 pandemic. The widespread fear of dying from the virus or of infecting loved ones, and the constant changes in priorities due to the uncertainty caused by the speed at which the virus spread.

In the early days of the war, there was chaos until some kind of order was introduced and there was constant uncertainty. The war became worldwide and Covid-19 became worldwide. The strain of prolonged uncertainty has another parallel – the adverse effect upon some peoples' mental health, particularly those who live alone.

There have been some positive results from having to live with Covid-19. For example, a renewed reliance upon each other and a coming together nationally to fully recover from the adversity. A greater appreciation of the NHS, particularly the frontline professionals, and an increased regard for those we take for granted too easily: postmen and women, delivery drivers, dustbin people. In general, all those folk who serve to provide us with a clean, happy and healthy life.

The vaccination of a vast proportion of the UK population as soon as possible was the turning point towards our lives returning to normality. Hitherto, the virus appeared to be ahead of the government reaction. All those involved in the vaccination distribution could take pride in their contribution, from design to delivery, and we can all be extremely thankful.

Let us look to the future positively, patriotically and with hope. I hope that sport plays an integral part in education so that the qualities of winning alongside how to deal with losing are taught in a meaningful way to support the mental health of future generations.

The advancements in technology, particularly in computerised communication and medicine, will surely continue. Computers in the early 1950s were the size of a very large wardrobe. Today, mobile devices have greater capacity and capability than the computer sat on my desk.

I look forward to seeing the continued growth of paraplegic sport, with proper funding and good facilities to attract participants and audiences alike.

Fortunately, there are signs that technological advances in the motor industry will enable hydrogen-fuelled engines, already in existence, to be produced in great numbers by 2040 – in time for the government's deadline on the ban in production of diesel and petrol cars. We can therefore look forward to having vehicles with emission systems that do not pollute the air we breathe, with sufficient evidence to give hope in reducing respiratory-related illness.

By nature, I am an outdoors person and have always enjoyed observing in detail what nature offers. If I need to clear my head for any reason, which is becoming more frequent with age, I take a walk outside at a pace that allows me to take in the immediate surroundings and the calls of the birds – starlings, jackdaws, robins and sparrows often make their presence known. The smell of freshly cut grass, the beautiful cherry blossom and the pendulous cream flowers of the chestnut trees. Collectively, they build a wonderful, restful atmosphere that simply puts life into perspective.

Finally, never underestimate the power you have to take your life in a different direction at any age.